DON'T EAT YOUR VOMIT!
WE ALL DO THIS
WRITTEN BY CAROLYN L. AUSTIN

Listening with a Different Ear

DON'T EAT YOUR VOMIT!

WE ALL DO THIS

WRITTEN BY CAROLYN L. AUSTIN

All Scripture quotations are taken from the Holy Bible, New International Version (NIV) Zondervan (Smart Phone Application) and the Holy Bible, King James Version (KJV) Tecarta, Inc. (Smart Phone Application), 2020-2021.

All anecdotes in this book recap real occurrences except for fictitious names, events, and places to protect the innocent and guilty.

Interior format: Carolyn L. Austin
Cover art: Mohsinwin, Fiverr.com

ISBN: 978-1-66781-887-0

Printed in the United States of America.

Dedication

This book is posthumously dedicated to my mother, Margaret, who passed away on December 16, 2020. I know she is with the Lord.

HOW TO USE THIS BOOK

Review of this book can be used for:

A Handbook Filled with Life Lessons

Managing and Purging Your Vomit

Self-Reflection

Inspiration

Enlightenment

Motivation

Empowerment

CONTENTS

CHAPTER 7

PART IV – The Third Quarter

CHAPTER 11

PREFACE

My mother told me, "Don't eat your vomit!" You see, my mother was referring to accepting people back into your life after they have done you wrong, broken your heart, or cheated on you. My tumultuous life experiences led me to also use "Don't eat your vomit" to refer to people I trusted, who later betrayed me so fiendishly that it felt as if they stabbed me in the back and twisted the knife.

When someone has wronged you, and you have given them opportunity upon opportunity to right their wrongs, and they have let you down every time - you are continuously eating your vomit by allowing them back into your life again and again. Can you imagine actually eating your own vomit? It would likely be an experience that you would not be eager to repeat and from which you would learn an invaluable lesson. Likewise, in life, when you allow those same people back into your life, it is like giving them a second bullet, because you survived their first one! You can always use the lessons you learn after you eat your vomit.

My mother's cautionary words, "You know, you don't eat your vomit," spoken at the demise of my first marriage, could be heard in my head again when I was at the same crossroad with my second marriage. I was in disbelief because I worked even harder to keep that marriage together. At some point, I remembered it was Scriptural.

2 Peter 2:19-22 NIV
[19] They promise them freedom, while they themselves are slaves of depravity---for "people are slaves to whatever has mastered them." [20] If they have escaped the corruption of the world by knowing our Lord and Savior Jesus Christ and are again entangled in it and are overcome, they are worse off at the end than they were at the beginning. [21] It would have been better for them not to have known the way of righteousness, than to have known it and then to turn their backs on the sacred command that was passed on to them. [22] Of them the

proverbs are true: "A dog returns to its vomit," and, "A sow that is washed returns to her wallowing in the mud."

More simply put,

Proverbs 26:11 NIV
[11] As a dog returns to its vomit, so fools repeat their folly.

My mother is the inspiration behind *Don't Eat Your Vomit!* Those words of wisdom were received with shock and awe, grabbing my attention amid a tumultuous time. They were later remembered when approaching that familiar moment of, "Do I stay, or do I go?" This book will force you to *recognize* don't-eat-your-vomit moments past or present – including those that do not necessarily involve a love relationship. *Don't Eat Your Vomit!* will help you *purge* or *manage* your vomit, since we all do this at least once, if not more, at some point in our lives.

ACKNOWLEDGMENTS

It is my pleasure to give formal appreciation to my editing team – Yeudele Allen, Marlené Carter, Deborah McCutchan, and Caroiya A. Williams, who tirelessly read and reread the content for *Don't Eat Your Vomit!* Each did not hesitate to encourage and support me while writing my story. Although, some did say, "Do you really want to do this?"

To my pre-readers – Anthenisia Austin Jackson, Paula Reeves, Carolyn Riggins, and Lisa Covins Sims; thank you for your constructive feedback.

To my focus group – Rhonda R. Dolby, Nell Holmes, Andrea Johnson, Arthurine Jones, Paulette Jones, Megan M. Lowe, and Fabiola P. Peck; thank you for your honest and heartfelt feedback.

I extend a special thanks to my daughter, Caroiya, who continues to encourage and support my writing endeavors – without criticism or judgment.

Thank you, ladies, for your commitment!

INTRODUCTION

I introduced the concept of "Don't Eat Your Vomit" in my first book, *Prayers of My Mother*. Since the book's completion in 2017, I have been overwhelmed and humbled by the emotional, heartfelt, and sincere impact *Prayers of My Mother* has had on the lives of others. Mostly, I continuously received questions about "Don't Eat Your Vomit."

Don't Eat Your Vomit! is the precursor to *Prayers of My Mother*. As I began writing this book, I saw how my journey lead directly to *Prayers of My Mother*. My path began with my mother, who was a prayer warrior. It was her prayers and healing ministry that catapulted me on this journey. But it was my trials and tribulations in the 80's and 90's that clarified my journey. During the '80s, I entered adulthood. I went to college and earned an associate degree. I landed my first job, married my high school sweetheart, gave birth to my one and only child, and divorced – all in four years. Before I divorced, I talked with my mother and expressed my disappointment regarding the state of my marriage, even changing my mind about divorce. She told me, "You know, you don't eat your vomit." Although I understood, it was not until years later that I recognized my vomit alluded to so much more – certain people, unhealthy relationships, and patterns of destructive behaviors.

Since then, *I* have returned to my vomit by remaining in a particular relationship – whether professional or personal to simply maintain my livelihood or fulfill a perceived desire or thirst. I have also danced around, purposely toyed with, and even bathed in it – believing these actions would satisfy some desire or quench my thirst. Even when dissatisfied or my thirst was unquenched, I embraced my vomit, yielding to the emotional rollercoaster and believing the outcome would change, only to be very disappointed in the end.

It is my desire that *"Don't Eat Your Vomit!"* helps you recognize or identify specific people, unhealthy relationships, and patterns of destructive behaviors in your life and teach how to deflect or cope with the consequences of returning to those same people, relationships, or patterns of destructive behaviors.

We all do this (eat our vomit) during our lifetime. Too many times, it is simply about perception. Some people learn after the first time, others continue their destructive cycle in hopes of changing the outcome. Rarely will they be successful.

In this book, I recount events in my adult life as I endured physical and emotional abuse while managing a successful, but challenging career. By allowing you to live vicariously through the choices I made and the corresponding mistakes, I pray it will assist you with *recognizing* and understanding your relationship and career vomit. Understanding is the key to preparing yourself to either *purge* or *manage* your vomit. Only then can you *survive* and *thrive*.

DON'T EAT YOUR VOMIT!
WE ALL DO THIS
WRITTEN BY CAROLYN L. AUSTIN

Warm-Up

Part I – Kick Off!

CHAPTER 1

First Love

In 1980, I earned my associate degree in business, which, at that time, was viewed much like bachelor's degrees are today. In early 1981, I got my first full-time job as an accounting clerk in the insurance industry. I remember being so happy and yelling to my mom and dad, "I got the job!" It only paid $10,000 a year. I cannot imagine making a living on that salary today. After working at the insurance company for approximately one year, I married Danny, my high school sweetheart.

Danny was cute as a button and *fine*! He was a bad boy, not a scholar like me. I guess it is true when they say opposites attract. My geometry teacher tried to warn me one day when she pulled me aside and said, "He is okay for *now*, but not later."

Although I did not listen to her, I have always remembered what she said about him.

The first time he hit me, we were in the front seat of his mother's car. We had just pulled into my parents' driveway. He distracted me by kicking my left foot and then used his hand to slap my left arm as I sat next to him. I cried immediately. After hitting me, he said, "You didn't cry because it hurt. You cried because I hit you."

I remember nodding my head, answering yes. I cannot precisely remember what motivated him to hit me, but I am sure he wanted me to do something that I would not or did not do. Besides, we were still in high school, and I did not give the hit much thought.

During our senior year in high school, Danny called me to say that his mother was dead. He explained that when he arrived home the night before, he thought she had fallen asleep in the chair as she had many times before. Danny said when he awoke the next morning, his mother was still in the chair. He further described shaking her body incessantly failing to wake her. Danny believed his mother had died the night before.

Danny and I had been dating for over a year, yet I had not met his mother. Although I knew where they lived, I had not gone inside their home. I remember once or twice seeing an elderly woman sitting on the porch. It was not until after Danny's mother passed away that I understood that the woman had been renting the left side of her house to Danny and his mother. The part of the house rented to them contained two rooms and a kitchen.

Danny always had a bunch of excuses when I asked to meet his mother. After we attended the Junior Prom, he told me that his mom had viewed our prom pictures. Danny said, "She likes you." I had no idea what she looked like until after she was deceased, and Danny showed me a picture. She was an obese woman with a nice smile. It occurred to me that he may have been embarrassed because of her size. My thoughts were confirmed years later once I had grown to learn Danny's superficiality.

Danny told me he had an older sister and brother who lived with their father in Georgia. It appeared that when Danny and his mother relocated to Florida, she left his father and siblings. I believed his mother married again because Danny mentioned his mother's last name, and it was different from his. Eventually, I met another man who was a father figure to Danny, although that man was married to someone else at the time.

Danny enrolled in night school and got a job after his mother's death. He did not attend night school for long before enlisting in the United States Army. His first duty station was in Heilbronn, Germany, where he obtained his high school equivalency diploma.

While Danny was away, I enrolled in Miami-Dade College with a full scholarship. The scholarship required maintaining a B average, and I graduated only a year and a half later with an associate degree. While in college, I hung out almost every weekend with my girlfriends at 8600 Big Daddy's, the local night club. Although I did not drink, I loved to dance. It was so much fun! Even when men occasionally approached me, it never occurred to me to date anyone else. After all, Danny was my first love, and I was extremely devoted to him. Isn't that how it is supposed to be?

When Danny returned home from Germany approximately a year later, he asked me to marry him. I was surprised at his proposal because I did not recall him mentioning marriage in any of the letters we exchanged while he was away. Being young and naive, I did not give marrying Danny a whole lot of thought. I was in love! As a matter of fact, I did not even remember that he hit me while we were in high school since he had not hit me again. I believed Danny was not only in love with me but that he deeply cared about me.

During the two weeks that Danny was home, he was persistent about our getting married. My eldest brother, Charles, visited me while I was deliberating Danny's proposal. Charles expressed reservations about my getting married, but when he saw I was determined and too stubborn to listen, he said apprehensively, "Okay." Charles' tone was something that I will never forget.

I finally gave in. Danny and I went to the courthouse and married on his birthday in February 1981. He was 20, and I was only 19! I did not know Danny's friends had been watching me while he was in Germany and giving him a full report of my social activities. Danny made several snide remarks about my partying with my friends. It was apparent he disapproved and wished he could control my choice in social activities.

He was only in Miami for approximately two weeks after we married. I quickly discovered that it was more than enough time to conceive when I began feeling differently, although I never experienced morning sickness. In less than one month after Danny returned to Germany, I learned I was pregnant.

Sometime after my first trimester of pregnancy, Danny advised in one of his letters that he would be stationed in Fort Polk, LA. I resigned from the insurance company after my second trimester and prepared to move to Louisiana. My family was extremely sad that I was leaving. I was sad too! However, I knew my responsibilities had changed. I had a husband and was expecting a child; therefore, it was time to start a life of my own.

I arrived at Fort Polk, LA, during my last trimester of pregnancy. Fort Polk was a culture shock in comparison to Miami, FL! Private first-class soldiers were not allowed to live on base because of their low position on the seniority list. To make matters worse, Danny was assigned to North Fort Polk instead of South Fort Polk. North Fort Polk was comprised of old, run-down looking buildings and structures. South Fort Polk had more newly constructed buildings. Even in 1981, it appeared that some areas of the military base remained segregated.

We moved to Leesville, LA, a small city bordering Fort Polk. Danny chose a small two-bedroom trailer located in a trailer park community at the perimeter of the military base. The only semblance to Miami was a mall located over two and a half hours southeast of Leesville in Baton Rouge, LA. Someone once commented that Fort Polk was the "armpit of the USA," and it was!

Initially, things seemed fine between Danny and me. Our first disagreement was in the commissary (grocery store). Danny thought I purchased too much of specific foods and household items. I was accustomed to purchasing items in bulk. Danny disagreed, which was evident as he walked around the store, putting the things I had placed in the shopping cart back on the shelves.

After leaving the store, he commented that people probably thought I was stupid because he put the items back. *That's not what they thought!* It was evident that people thought Danny did not want to spend the money on the bulk items.

During my last month of pregnancy, I purchased a car seat for the baby. Danny complained about the car seat purchase and demanded that I take it back to the store. He claimed that the baby did not need a car seat. I refused to return it. Until this day, I am still baffled about Danny's reasoning. Was it because the car seat cost $100? Was he stupid, cheap or both?

The day my water broke, I had just returned from buying a compact crib for the baby. I thought the water was a little urine since the baby had begun to press on my bladder. After all, it was my first time being pregnant, and I missed my scheduled Lamaze class in Miami. I was unaware of amniotic fluid warnings and other necessary information. Oblivious, I continued my evening as usual and slept without discomfort. It was not until I arrived at my scheduled doctor's appointment on the following morning and mentioned the urine incident that a litmus paper test was performed confirming I was in danger of infection. The doctor told me, "You need to have the baby *now*!"

"But I'm not ready!" I exclaimed.

The staff instructed me to walk around the waiting room to encourage contractions. *If contractions had not started after a full night's sleep, why would they start after I walked?* When walking around did not jump-start my contractions, I was given the drug Pitocin to induce labor. The Pitocin pushed me into advanced labor pains in what seemed like zero to 60 seconds! I advised the doctor in advance that I did not want any drugs to ease the pain because they could affect the baby. But, after experiencing extreme labor pain so quickly, I relented. However, the drugs did not take effect until *after*

I delivered a beautiful, healthy baby girl! Before showing me my baby, I heard one of the nurses say, "What beautiful eyes!"

When Danny arrived at my room soon after I delivered, he said, "She has ten little fingers and ten little toes."

What an idiot! Then I passed out from the effects of whatever that pain reliever was. When I finally awoke, my mother was sitting at my bedside. My first words to her were, "How could you do this six times?"

She responded, "You forget."

The first four months with Danny after the baby was born were barely tolerable. Danny had the nerve to ask me why she was so light, referring to her skin complexion. "My mother is fair-skinned!" I snapped. *Idiot!* Danny complained when the baby cried, impatient to allow me to console her. Once, on a cold winter night, he pushed the bassinette into the hallway because she would not stop crying, and he could not sleep. I cried, quickly learning to sleep in the other room. Crying became normal for me because Danny behaved so irrationally.

I finally went to Miami to see my family when my baby was four months old. It felt great to be home and with my two sisters who were overjoyed about meeting their niece for the very first time. My older sister was astonished to see that the baby's eyes were blue. I thought they were gray. My baby's eyes were actually hazel. Once, I watched them change colors right before my eyes after giving her a piece of candy. It was so cool! It was much later that I remembered praying to the Lord while pregnant, asking that my baby have hazel eyes. Hazel eyes were something I admired. He answered my prayer!

My father thought my baby looked just like me when I was her age. They were all amazed that she was not a whining baby. I knew it was because I nursed her. Danny called me every day, begging me to return to Louisiana. I abruptly ended my visit with my family because he would not allow me to enjoy my visit with them in peace.

A distinctive chain of events occurred over the next few months. The minor details are blurred, but the effects are painfully ingrained in my heart forever. First, before my baby could sit up on her own, I left her with Danny while I went to the store with a neighbor. When I returned, my baby had a red bruise on the side of her face. As I sat down on the bed bewildered, asking Danny what happened to her, he responded that he did not know. He acted as if the red mark miraculously appeared on her face. Forever in my memory is my baby looking up at me from that bassinette like she wanted to tell me what happened.

A day or so later, with my baby strapped to my chest in her papoose, I walked to the convenience store located at the trailer park entrance. An Asian woman stopped to see my baby and motioned toward the bruise on her face, "What happened?" she asked in broken English. I shrugged my shoulders in response. She said, "Bottle?"

I reflected on the glass bottles I filled with powdered formula when supplementing my breast milk, which I had supplied for Danny on that day. *Maybe that is what happened.* However, I did not leave my baby with Danny again.

On another day, I wanted to go to the hospital to see my neighbor after she had her baby. Danny argued with me about something which I cannot remember and slapped me in my face. It could have been that he did not want me to go to the hospital. Despite his slapping me, I took my baby with me to the hospital to see my neighbor. As I sat next to my neighbor's hospital bed, she looked at me sympathetically and commented, "I know Dan is giving you a hard time."

When my baby was around seven months old, Danny sat her in the car's front passenger seat without strapping her in the seat belt. Of course, the car seat was in the car, but he obviously did not use it. He seemed somewhat amused when reporting (after I questioned him about another red mark on her body), that when he returned from going into the store to pay for the gas, he found her on the car's passenger side floor. Danny reacted like she was supposed to understand how to sit still on the seat and not fall.

The last time I remember being on the receiving end of his anger was when he picked me up and dropped me on the trailer's floor! I recall that my baby was sitting on the couch. I cannot remember the reason for that abusive episode either. But I do remember lying on the floor, very confused about how our relationship had evolved to that point. After that day, it seemed that I learned to recognize Danny's triggers because I do not recall any other similar incidents while in Fort Polk.

Eventually, I got a job, and things seemed to get better at home. My neighbor kept my baby while I worked at a stereo shop, part of a chain of stores erected around military bases. My opportunity to escape from Fort Polk came when my mother phoned to tell me that Florida International University (FIU) had written to advise me that I needed to enroll in school by the 1982 Fall Term or lose the scholarship. I had previously gained a full scholarship opportunity from FIU as an extension of my Miami-Dade College scholarship program. At that time, the Fall Term was right around the corner, and there was no way I could return to Miami in time to attend. I spoke with someone in registration and was allowed to enroll in the 1983 Winter Term instead. I then recommended my neighbor for my job at the stereo shop and prepared to return to Miami. My baby was ten months old.

Danny and I drove back to Miami with my baby in her car seat in the backseat. When it was my turn to drive, I was falling asleep while driving. I was awakened when I heard my name spoken in a quiet but very audible voice. When I opened my eyes, I was alarmed to see that I was ascending a bridge. Once I drove over the bridge, I pulled into the very first rest stop I encountered and went to sleep. When Danny awoke, he began yelling at me because we were parked at a rest stop. He believed it dangerous to sleep at rest stops. It was clear that Danny had not awakened me. My only choices were to stop to sleep or risk the lives of everyone in the car if I had fallen asleep again.

The plan for returning to Miami while Danny re-enlisted in the Army was to live with my parents, attend school full-time, and complete my bachelor's degree. I knew we should be on our own. So, I began searching for an apartment. The rental rates were about $500 a month. I learned that we could buy a home and pay the same amount for a monthly mortgage payment. Therefore, I began looking for houses.

I believed that if Danny remained in the Army, he would mature, and our marriage could survive. I learned that while Danny was in Germany, he received "too many Article 15s," and as a result, was not allowed to re-enlist. An Article 15 meant he committed some minor misconduct which led to his commanding officer's disciplinary action. Perhaps, if Danny had only one Article 15, he may have been able to remain in the Army. His admitting to having "too many" likely meant that he had two or more minor misconduct infractions. Combining them, I surmise, probably made him an undesirable candidate for another term. Whatever Danny did or did not do, he had to return to Miami too! So, the plan changed because we both had to work. I was not allowed to be a part-time student and fulfill the scholarship requirements. Therefore, I enrolled in college with a full-time course schedule and a full-time job, attempting to maintain a B average to keep the scholarship.

Before my first semester at FIU, I was scheduled to take an exam used to evaluate new students. In essence, I was a guinea pig for a new testing process. The night before the exam, Danny came in late after hanging out with his homeboy Willie, an excuse I was given often. Danny would not let me sleep. Each time I closed my eyes, he would wake me by shaking my body or touching me in my face. It was extremely irritating! As a result, I took the exam without any sleep. I am sure my scores could have been better if I had slept the night before. I did not learn until years later that his behavior mirrored someone high on drugs. He could not sleep, so he did not allow me to sleep either.

When I began job hunting, I contacted my old manager at the insurance company. Initially, there were no positions available. But in less than a month, she called me when a position became available. I began working for the insurance company again. Danny eventually got a job as a driver for a local business. We only had one car, but somehow, we managed.

One morning, I was getting ready for work, and Danny did not want me to drive the car because he was off that day and wanted to keep it. We began to argue. I cannot exactly remember if he pushed or hit me, but I exploded and began to fight back. He tried to control my flailing arms and legs by attempting to pin me down on the bed. But the force and pressure he used to control me somehow landed on the left side of my face and left eye. It was very painful. When I managed to get up, I grabbed my high heeled shoe with my right hand and commenced to putting a high heel sized hole in his left arm. At this point, he just stood there, and I yelled at him, "Get out!"

The left side of my face and left eye swelled instantaneously. Upon looking in the mirror, it looked as if Danny punched me in the eye. My eye and face were red. My lower eyelid was puffy because fluid had begun to accumulate in the area. As I laid on the bed, my 11-month-old baby reached out to touch my left eye. I remember thinking how smart she was to see that my eye did not look normal. When I returned to work the next day – yes, I went to work, I told everyone I walked into a door. I am sure no one believed me.

My father convinced me to let ·Danny come back to my parents' home. He said that a married man should not be out in the street. By this time, I was taking college courses in the evening. My mother, a registered nurse at a local hospital, had the benefit of utilizing the hospital's daycare. It was such a blessing that my baby could attend a daycare located at a hospital. My baby arrived in the mornings, and it was Danny's responsibility to pick her up in the evenings. One evening after school, I came home to discover that my baby was still at the daycare. It was 10:00 p.m.! When I asked Danny why he would leave her there for over 12 hours, he said, "I am too young to babysit."

I retorted, "You weren't too young to lay down and have sex to conceive her!"

One evening, Danny was supposed to keep the baby. By this time, my baby was about 15 months old. When I prepared her for a bath that night, I noticed she had this strangely shaped mark on her right forearm, and its edges were round. It resembled what I thought a cigarette burn would look like after it had begun to heal. The area was not red. I asked Danny where he had been that evening. He said he was at Willie's place.

Willie lived with his girlfriend, whom I only met once. She was a thin, unattractive girl whose lips were noticeably dark. She was smoking a cigarette when I met her, and I believed she smoked marijuana too. No way could we be friends! The only thing we had in common was Danny and Willie. Danny told me he allowed Willie's girlfriend to keep my baby while he and Willie hung out. I knew it was not the first time.

"DO NOT – LEAVE – MY BABY WITH HER AGAIN!" I said sternly and with emphasis. *You irresponsible idiot!*

After that first semester, I lost the scholarship. I was unable to maintain a B average and work full-time in conjunction with having no reliable and responsible support from Danny. It was for the best because he was incapable of being a decent father. Danny just did not know how.

At work, I became motivated to get promoted and make more money, especially since we were house hunting. I received a couple of promotions while at the insurance company and earned an additional $1,000-$2000 a year. When the insurance company relocated a little over an hour farther south, they created a shuttle service. Danny would drop me off at the park 'n ride in the mornings and pick me up in the evenings. One day when Danny picked me up, the song, "Every Breath You Take" by The Police, sung by the infamous Sting, had just finished playing on the radio. Perhaps Danny received an unspoken vibe from me when he repeated a line from the lyrics and said, "Remember, 'I'll be watching you.'" It was very spooky because although I had not made a firm decision yet, I was contemplating leaving Danny.

We began the home buying process after choosing a two-bedroom home, which was all we could afford. I phoned my second oldest brother, Winston, who was an attorney in Georgia. I told him that Danny and I were not getting along, and I did not think buying a home together was a good idea. Winston said backing out would ruin my credit. He told me to buy the house and "Put the *N-word* out!" I chuckled and decided to continue with the home buying process. However, I made a promise to myself that Danny had one more time to hit or hurt me.

We moved into our new home in late August or early September 1983. My baby would have been about 21 months old. In retrospect, maybe I thought Danny could be the young man with whom I had fallen in love. It seemed that Danny was better with me before he joined the military. But Danny joined the Army Reserves after being discharged from the Army and was required to go to the field once every two months or so. Therefore, if the military atmosphere was supposed to mature him, it was not working. It only took a month for Danny to show me that he could not change for the better.

I am sure my enthusiasm for sex with Danny changed tremendously. I remember his asking me, "Why do you like that song when you don't like sex?" This question was in response to my singing along as the radio DJ played Marvin Gaye's "Sexual Healing." I was unsure if Danny had some new sexual fantasy or was high one evening when he stuck his middle finger into my rectum. He did not ask my permission, and I felt violated. The look on his face appeared to be some sort of scowl. After that night, I planned my escape.

I knew that telling Danny I was leaving would not be a good idea because he would try to prevent me from leaving. Therefore, I decided to leave him during the upcoming duty weekend scheduled for October (1983). I began gathering my things before the October weekend to make it easier for me to leave when the time came. It was then that I noticed some of my things were missing. I had a small, compact 12" black and white TV and some jewelry items that were no longer in the closet where I kept them.

A day or so after my discovery, Danny mistakenly left his wallet on top of the fireplace. It was then that I again heard that quiet but very audible voice tell me to look inside his wallet. I had never gone into his wallet before. But upon looking inside, I found several pawnshop tickets describing the items I had been searching for. The severity of the situation had not quite settled in as I angrily went to the pawnshop to retrieve my things. After much discussion with the pawnshop owner, and a return trip to the pawnshop with signed pawnshop tickets, I finally recovered my things. Among my things was his wedding band, which was supposed to be lost. I took the items to my parents' house. I returned home and gathered the remainder of my things and my baby's things, and we moved back home with my parents.

While at my parents' home, I wondered why Danny would pawn my things for money. We both worked. Danny also gave me his paycheck each pay period to pay the bills and household expenses. When Danny phoned my parents' home looking for me, he asked me when I was coming home. I told him, "I'm not coming home!"

I explained that I found the pawnshop tickets and retrieved my things along with his wedding band. I asked him why he needed money. The question went unanswered. However, there was no answer that Danny could have given me to convince me to return to our home.

It was during this time that I talked to my mother about divorcing Danny. I am not sure what I said to my mother exactly. So much had happened between Danny and me. I gave the marriage so much effort, even forgot the abuse I endured while living in Louisiana. Danny's stupidity and carelessness with my baby was pure serendipity. I methodically eliminated a need for him to keep my baby. In retrospect, it was ludicrous to go to those lengths. Perhaps, my mother sensed my thoughts from the expression on my face. She said, "You know, you don't eat your vomit!" Time stood still as I pondered my mother's meaning. It was a moment that I will never forget.

After about two months, I returned to the home we shared to speak with Danny about his not paying the mortgage. Upon entering the house, something did not feel right. I asked him if someone was there. He said, *no*. I walked towards the two bedrooms, looking into the opened door of the baby's room, and then reaching for the doorknob of the master bedroom, but decided not to open it. I turned around and walked toward the dining room table, sitting down across from Danny.

I noticed his behavior was oddly familiar. As I observed him for a few moments, I remembered that he behaved in the same manner when I questioned him about the red mark on my baby's face when she was only five months old, looking up at me from the bassinette. Instantly, I knew Danny had hit my baby, probably because she would not stop crying. Based on my observation, I also knew that I could finally characterize his behavior as guilt, and that there was someone in the master bedroom. Those moments sealed the fate of our marriage. I told him he needed to leave the house if he would not pay the mortgage, and I departed.

I separated from Danny and began looking for another job. I bought a car from someone who also worked at the insurance company. I began insisting that Danny move out of our house when a co-worker and I discussed becoming roommates. She was also separated and had filed for divorce. I hired her attorney to help me with my divorce.

It was a sunny day in Miami during April 1984, when Danny and I finally divorced. I recall being in court when the judge ordered Danny to pay child support or go to jail immediately. Danny had not paid me any money since I had left him six months prior. As we departed the courthouse, Danny said, "You were going to let them put me in jail?" Then he told me, "You're not going to find anyone else." In response, I looked at him in disgust. I could have pushed him down the courthouse steps!

When I arrived at my parents' home, my baby came running through the carport and down the driveway to greet me. I picked her up into the air and said, "We're free!"

My father, watching us from the front door, said, "Don't do it again, unless you are sure."

Instant Replay

It took me several years to recognize that Danny had manipulated me in the worst way. The primary reason that Danny wanted us to marry and have a baby was not only to keep me from meeting someone else while he was in Heilbronn, Germany but to also tie me down with the responsibility of a baby. In his mind, I was this good girl, and going to the night club regularly ruined his image of me. He thought it was the perfect plan to control me and my social activities. Whenever I arrived at the realization of Danny's motives, I gained a new perspective of him. The concept of my marriage was no longer the great love story that I believed it to be.

The marriage evolved into an abusive situation after my baby was born. Should I have been able to discern that Danny slapping me on the arm while sitting in the front seat of his mother's car when we were teenagers would become an abusive relationship? Danny treated the baby like she was my favorite toy doll that got more attention than he did. He acted like breaking my doll would get him the attention he sought. Danny was jealous of his own child and behaved stupidly. His carelessness in handling her were acts of defiance. I did not think I was giving Danny less attention at all. I was just taking care of our baby. However, the more he mistreated her and put her in vulnerable situations, the more I began to hate him.

Danny once told me, "You always say, 'my child!'" He never treated her the way I thought a man should treat "his" child. Danny appeared to resent our child's place in our lives, which would always be ahead of him. He was the adult, and she was just a baby. His scheme to possess and control me backfired because he underestimated what having a baby would mean in not only our marriage but in our lives!

At that time, it was so difficult for me to *recognize* that I was allowing *vomit* to live and thrive in my life while living in Fort Polk, LA. I kept trying to fix everything, desperately wanting to give Danny a chance to be someone he just could not be. Each time he was careless with my baby, I established a new boundary to protect her. It was like taking a privilege from a child because they abused it. First, it was not leaving her with Danny anymore after she was five months old and then taking her everywhere with me because he refused to use the car seat. Next, it was leaving her at the daycare longer on the nights I had school since he refused to be responsible for her wellbeing. I tried to protect my child by continuously readjusting the boundaries I set for Danny until there were no longer any adjustments to make.

It never occurred to me that I should leave Danny when we were in Louisiana. Perhaps my respect for the institution of marriage had been instilled in me by my parents. But returning to Miami gave me the reprieve I needed from my previous living conditions and allowed me to recognize that I had my family's support. I am sure that had I told my parents that I wanted to leave Fort Polk, I could have been on the next plane back to Miami. I remember calling my mother once to tell her Danny and I were fighting. But I never told her again, mostly because I did not want her to worry about me. Now that I am older and wiser, I believe it was also because I had to handle things on my own and not quit.

When we had that final fight at my parents' house, I made a promise to myself that I would not live with him as I had in Louisiana, and I kept that promise when I removed myself and my child from his life. It was not until many years later that I even remembered the unexplainable voice I heard while driving from Louisiana and before finding the pawnshop tickets. When I did remember, I knew it was the Spirit of the Lord intervening and redirecting my path to fulfill His plans for my life.

[11] *For I know the plans I have for you," declares the Lord, "plans to prosper you and not to harm you, plans to give you hope and a future. (Jeremiah 29:11 NIV)*

My mother's words summed it all up for me that day. I had indeed been wallowing in my vomit. I am sure some women would have probably been arrested and jailed several times after enduring what I had and defending themselves against men like Danny. I am not sure what the laws were then, but my younger self did not think about that. I operated in the moment of trusting my own judgment and doing my best to survive for my child and me. I was not going to be hauled away because I lost control. Knowing the law as I do now, losing control in a situation like that could have resulted in several undesirable outcomes. Specifically, if I had not seriously injured Danny or killed him in a moment of rage, he could have been the guardian of my child!

Prayer:
Father, we come to You on bent knees for the people who have experienced abusive relationships, whether physical, verbal, or psychological. Lord, give us the strength to see that a positive solution is possible. Help us to know that You will show us what we need to see when we need to see it. Father, You are there even when we are not praying, when we are picking ourselves up off the ground and hurting because we overlooked the characteristics of our mates, those we cannot change. Lord, forgive us and help us to forgive ourselves when we are too trusting. Father, please help us to heal when we are still angry with ourselves for what we have endured. Lord, we know that You will not give us more than we can handle, show us how we can minister to one another to reveal the strength that only You can give. Father, we thank You in advance for the victory. Lord, we love You, and we praise Your holy name, in Jesus' name we pray, amen.

Part II – The First Quarter

CHAPTER 2

Huddle

In April 1984, I read an advertisement in the newspaper about a junior accountant position at a large security company that paid $15,000 a year. The prerequisite for the job was having an accounting background and associate degree. The security company was half the distance away from my home than the insurance company, which made my commute forty-five minutes less. I interviewed for the position and was hired. Life was good!

After working there for a few months, I received a notice in the mail advising that I was still eligible for a position with the Postal Service, and they were hiring again. I was on a list of candidates who had previously taken and passed the postal entry exam in 1980. I took a deductive reasoning approach when completing the exam and barely passed it. I later learned there were classes available to prepare for the exam to ensure high scores and increase hiring odds. After further inquiry, I determined a postal position would provide excellent benefits. It was the same distance from my home as the security company but in the opposite direction. Not to mention the Postal Service was paying $24,000 a year! The prospect of an increased salary and good benefits made my decision to leave the security company relatively easy. So, I resigned and began working for the Postal Service.

Truthfully, I hated working for the Postal Service. I tearfully complained about the job to my mother every night. She told me it would get better. I had traded my professional attire and office for blue jeans and a workroom floor. I regretted it! At that time, I could not have imagined working there for an additional five years – let alone 33 years, but I did. It was a journey filled with significant learning moments that will remain with me for the rest of my life.

I began my career in the Postal Service as a part-time employee, working evening and overnight shifts, which was how most postal employees started. Many people did not like me because I was quiet. However, I quickly learned to speak up to prevent being taken advantage of by lazy full-time employees. The full-timers left all the work for the part-timers. Eventually, I made friends, and the job became tolerable.

Even though I was a part-time employee, there was plenty of work. I rarely worked less than 8 hours. It was manual labor, requiring acute memorization skills for some areas. The part-time and full-time job assignments required schemes – memorizing addresses, ZIP codes, and carrier routes. There was a tremendous amount of stress that accompanied being a part-time employee. I studied every night to pass the qualifying test for my first assignment. If I had not memorized my assignments, I would have been fired!

I was hired with a group of people who were sometimes assigned to work in the same areas as I did. Some of us developed friendships. Initially, I was assigned the evening shift, working from 3:30 p.m. to 12 a.m. Others were assigned the night shift, working from 9:30 p.m. to 6:00 a.m. It was during that two-and-a-half-hour overlap that I met James. He worked nights.

CHAPTER 3

The Womanizer

During that overlap, James initiated a conversation with me in the breakroom. I thought he was handsome and incredibly charming. I liked him immediately! James would sometimes meet me near the training room, after I studied and practiced keying on the replicated mail processing machine. We eventually exchanged numbers and began communicating outside of work.

James would pick me up for lunch after he had taken his morning nap. I believed he was scholarly after he and I discussed taking a college-level calculus course. It was a welcome contrast to my ex-husband. He also introduced me to singer/songwriter Kashif's music – who is still one of my favorites today. Even though James was a few years older, I was excited to date someone college-educated and mature – so I thought.

One day we returned to my house after having lunch. We were standing in my living room, facing each other. I was looking up at James with starry-eyed wonderment when he said, "When you want to get married?"

Even though it was an unexpected question, I blurted out, "June!"

I was so infatuated with him. We were not sexually active, and that made me feel even more special! He treated me like it was love at first sight. I guess I needed to believe in a fairy tale after being treated horribly during my failed marriage. I thought surely six months was more than enough time to plan a wedding.

I had met his mother, but she was not as warm and friendly as I would have liked or expected. James only introduced me by my name, absent of any crucial qualifiers like girlfriend or fiancée. The look on his mother's face screamed, "Here is another one!" But I ignored his mother.

Immediately, I began dreaming about this bad (as in *absolutely* gorgeous) dress I would make. I knew I could sew something that would be the envy of everyone. Sewing was something I learned by watching my mother at the age of 10. I began shopping for sewing patterns, looking for the perfect dress – only Vogue patterns would do! I chose purple as the wedding color. Although I had been married before, I still wanted to wear white. I planned to make it *pop* by inserting layers of sheer purple and sheer white fabric when making the skirt of the wedding dress. Yes, I was preparing to plan the most beautiful wedding, especially since I had not had one before.

One night after work, as I exited the building through the doors leading to the parking lot, I saw someone in the shadows, wearing dark-colored clothing, lurking near the exit doors. I was startled when the person approached me and asked, "Are you dating James?"

It was a woman and I bewilderedly answered, "Yes."

She continued, "I'm dating him!"

Deannie, my co-worker, pulled me along as if saving me from a physical confrontation. She was also in the group that was hired with me. Deannie and I were together often and usually assigned the same areas to work. She was five or so years older than me. Deannie spoke to me like I was naïve and seemed to act as if she was my big sister. She said the woman's name was Stacy, and that Stacy worked the night shift. So, when I saw James the following day, I explained what happened the night before. He responded, "Stacy is dating Dave."

Obviously, it was not what Stacy thought. I knew she would not have approached me if James had not done something to make her feel or believe they were dating. But James offered no plausible explanation regarding Stacy's assertion. Frankly, his response that

Stacy and Dave were dating was an attempt to get the focus off him, which did not explain Stacy approaching me.

Soon after, I began receiving sideways glances from others. I was sure it was because something was going on between James and Stacy. Since I was not on the night shift, I was not privy to any clarifying information, and no one volunteered to enlighten me. I also knew that my so-called big-sister and friend, Deannie, had some pertinent information that she was not sharing with me.

I soon began hearing about other women that James was allegedly seeing. I knew that if James was serious about me, there would not have been a Stacy or anyone else. Was this a game that James often played with women, cavalierly putting thoughts of marriage in their heads? It appeared a form of manipulation James used to convince women he was serious about them.

During this time, Cookie, my childhood friend, who was also my second roommate, provided support with my daughter while I worked in the evenings. We discussed James and his proposal of marriage to me. As we plotted, Cookie suggested that I tell James I mailed wedding invitations. We believed that upon telling him I mailed invitations, he would admit that he was not serious about his proposal. But when I told James about the invitations, he did not even seem surprised. As a matter of fact, he said nothing. I expected a question regarding his tentative guest list or something. On the contrary, he appeared to want to believe I was just that stupid. I am not sure why I let him think that I mailed invitations. However, James did stop calling me, but not for long.

Some months passed, and James started calling me again. I can only imagine that he had run through his options on the night shift and wanted my attention again. By this time, Deannie had also been assigned to the night shift. Periodically, she would call me to spread information or attempt to get information. I was always careful about what I shared with Deannie. Once, I purposely mentioned to Deannie that James had stopped by my house one morning, and she appeared to be a little jealous, wanting details which I would not provide. Listening to Deannie, James was quite the womanizer. She seemed to take pleasure in informing me about whomever James was supposedly dating.

One day, James stopped by my house. By this time, my daughter was about three years old. She was with me that day and not at my parents' home, where she normally would have been. When James entered my house, he greeted my daughter by picking her up and calling her name, feigning affection. His attention so tickled my daughter! I was sure she would remember James after that performance.

James' conversation with me did not include any type of apology for playing with my feelings. I am sure he had not given much thought to anything he had said to me regarding our getting married. I, on the other hand, did not appreciate his callous indifference. I had moved past that moment; although, I thought myself naïve for believing his rhetoric. It was a fundamental lesson for me to learn about (some) men.

Somehow, our conversation led to James telling me about his two children from different women. James said he had a girl and a boy and told me their names. I remember the girl was about 8 or 10 years old, and the boy was around 3 years old. For some reason, I asked James if they (calling their names) were the only two children he had. He answered, *yes*. James appeared to want us to date again. I could not help but notice the sincerity he exhibited when he talked about the children. So, I decided to let things play out between us.

A couple of days after that conversation with James, I learned what an even bigger liar he was. It was rare that I picked up my daughter from school because I was usually working. The school was in the heart of Miami, and the teachers had done an excellent job with my baby. Just after I retrieved my daughter from the classroom and began walking away, one of her teachers ran behind me and handed me a small envelope. It was an invitation for a child's birthday party. The teacher expressed wanting my daughter to attend.

I thought it very strange that a teacher would invite one of her 3-year-old students to their child's birthday party. My curiosity heightened. I opened the invitation while walking out of the school. My mouth dropped wide open as I read the invitation. The party was for a one-year-old, and her last name was the same as James'. *Oh, my God!*

When I arrived home, I told Cookie what happened. "Can you believe that I just asked James when he was here the other day if he only had the two children, and he said, 'yes!'"

Cookie exclaimed, "Girl, go to that party!" Then she added, "You know how kids talk."

That's exactly what happened! My baby more than likely mentioned to her teacher that her mommy had a boyfriend named James. As I contemplated attending the party, I thought it a good idea. I believed it would end James' charade with me, especially after he had told me that bold-faced lie about the number of children he had. So, I attended the party.

When I arrived at the park's pavilion where the party was being held, James' mother looked at me and whispered something to her husband. *Messy old woman!* I made sure my daughter and I dressed well. I approached my daughter's teacher and handed her a store-wrapped gift containing two pretty dresses. I smiled as I encouraged her to shop at JC Penney, and explained the store was having a great sale. She looked at me, incredulously. I am sure she did not expect me to attend the party. I realized her *only* purpose for inviting me was to advise that James was her baby's daddy. But I used the party invitation to *my* advantage! Not only did I show James that he was busted, but also that I did not care about him – which I perfectly demonstrated as I walked right past him without speaking! James was in utter disbelief that I was there.

My daughter and I walked through the pavilion and headed for the swings and slide located behind it. Once my daughter played for a couple of minutes, I took her hand and said, "Let's go, baby!" No one said anything to us for the entire fifteen minutes or so that we were at the party. But I am sure they were all staring at us.

I thought it despicable that James did not claim or acknowledge his child. I have always believed that children do not ask to be here, so we should be kind to them and show them love. Perhaps James thought admitting having a third child (who was probably a newborn when I met him) would somehow make him less desirable. He was already undesirable because he was such a liar! I had finally entertained James' lies for the very last time because he stopped calling me after the party.

Several months later, I learned that one of James' children had died suddenly. By this time, I was not sure how many children James had fathered. It had not occurred to me that the baby who had died was the same baby whose party I attended. It was not until I was walking toward the postal credit union that my daughter's teacher was in my path. She was sitting on the brick-layered knee wall, located at the post office, near the credit union's employee entrance. I gasped, "That was your baby?"

She responded, "Yes, that was my baby."

"I'm so sorry," I said softly.

Then I looked up to see James coming towards us, and I quickly walked away, saying nothing to him. *Oh, my Lord!* My mind continued to race as I shook my head. *What an idiot! He did not even claim that baby.*

A couple of years later, I learned James believed my lie about mailing invitations for our fictitious wedding. I was told by a new employee who liked me enough to inform me that people were still talking and laughing behind my back. She said they were discussing how I mailed invitations for a wedding that obviously never happened. I could not believe that James would tell people what I told him. But I guess since he was the liar and not me, he believed me. I found it more interesting that his gigantic ego caused him to spread a rumor that I created!

I called Deannie and asked her if she knew of a rumor about me mailing wedding invitations. Deannie told me she did, and she could not believe that I was just finding out. *Heifer! I knew she wasn't my friend!* Deannie was laughing behind my back too. I still laugh about the lie Cookie encouraged me to tell James. It was intended to check him but eventually revealed his lack of integrity. The entire ordeal confirmed the type of man James was and the lack of maturity he possessed.

Ladies' Man

The Postal Service was not all work and no play. There were many formal dinners and dances for different occasions. Each time a formal function was scheduled, I would buy fabric and make an original dress so that no one else could wear what I wore. However, for my very first function, I wore a dress I purchased from Macy's. It was a cream-colored dress with a fitted bodice and puffy short sleeves, worn off the shoulders. The skirt of the dress had pink appliques. Today, this dress may sound old-fashioned, but this was around 1985. I was only 24 years old, and I thought the dress was perfect!

Cookie had braided my hair with extensions a week or so before the function. Instead of taking the braids out, we decorated my hair with pastel-colored dressmaker pins. We stuck the pins in between the braids and evenly spaced them at the beginning of each braid, about a half-inch away from my hairline, gently framing my face and being careful not to stick my scalp. As a result, my hair had the appearance of having tiny pearls sprinkled strategically throughout. It was beautiful! Since it was my first postal function, I was not sure what to expect. As anticipated, no one's dress or hair was similar to mine!

My first encounter with Freddie was after the dance. I knew of him because he was a supervisor on the night shift. Freddie was thin, kind of handsome, and extremely confident. He had a nice smile. Freddie was also charming, quick-witted, and well-liked by most. My lunch buddy, outside of most, said he could not stand Freddie.

When I departed the banquet room, I explored the hotel. While walking in the passageways, I sensed I was being followed. When I looked behind me, Freddie was there, but not too close. I startled him when I abruptly turned around and caught him in the act! I giggled, *Yeah, he's following me.* But he did not say anything, so I kept walking.

After working evenings for approximately one year, my daughter was almost four years old. I thought the arrangement with Cookie and my parents worked quite well, but I sensed my daughter needed more attention from me. My happy little baby's behavior had begun to change, and she was very much resistant to my authority. I believed it was because she spent more time with Cookie and my parents and not enough time with me. I decided to submit a temporary change of schedule, requesting either the day or night shift. I believed that if I could be home in the evenings and put my baby to bed, it would help our relationship. Although I requested days, only people with seniority worked the day shift, which began at 6:00 a.m. So, I knew the only change of schedule that would be granted for me was nights. As predicted, my schedule was changed to nights. Consequently, I worked the night shift for approximately three months.

Working nights for those three months was quite an adjustment. My neighbor mowed his lawn late one morning, just as I fell asleep. Once awakened, I was unable to return to sleep. I suffered at work that night because I could not keep my eyes open.

My stomach was in knots from pure exhaustion. I continuously walked to the bathroom, trying to stay awake. I even tried to get a nap in one of the stalls, hoping that a few minutes of sleep would allow me to make it through the night. After that night, I learned to close the windows and lower the shades to block out the noise and light, making the bedroom conducive for sleeping. Eventually, my body adjusted, and I was able to sleep during the day and function at night.

While on evenings, I worked what was called outgoing mail. The night shift usually worked incoming mail and I was assigned another scheme to learn. This time, I was not required to pass the scheme as a condition of my employment. Learning a new scheme simply enabled me to be more productive while working nights. When I was ready to be tested on the incoming mail scheme, the supervisor assigned to monitor and test me was Freddie.

Upon entering the test room, Freddie seemed surprised to see me there. Judging by his reaction, he was unaware of my change of schedule. After the test, Freddie said I did not pass. I was confident I had, and I am sure that the look on my face showed confusion. Then Freddie quickly admitted that I had passed and laughed at his attempt to tease me. I knew he was taking advantage of finally having the opportunity to talk with me.

One night, soon after passing my test, while I was sitting at my mail case working the incoming mail, Freddie approached me and asked, "Would you like to see me?"

I had never been asked on a date in that manner. I assumed that Freddie was asking me on a date. I smiled a little and answered *yes* by nodding my head. Due to Freddie's reputation, I knew he would probably ask if I wanted to sleep with him. We planned to meet one morning after work.

Also, while on evenings, I had heard many stories about Freddie. I was not oblivious to his reputation. He was extremely popular with the women. As a matter of fact, Freddie was a ladies' man. Freddie was not as pretentious as James had been. Women often gossiped what they "heard" about the size of Freddie's manhood. There was also chatter that his house had a revolving door, meaning that as one woman entered the front door, another would be leaving out the back door. It was quite melodramatic, but I was curious.

My decision to meet with Freddie was one that I made with my eyes WIDE OPEN! I had no commitment expectations of Freddie. After Danny and James, I decided that I would control whatever my next relationship would be. I had to admit that the gossip alone was a forewarning, indeed! Therefore, I demanded full disclosure from Freddie and disclose he did – sometimes more than I wanted!

We finally met one morning after work at a local hotel. Since I did not disagree to meeting there, I accepted the direction in which we were headed. Freddie chose the hotel and gave me the address. I arrived first, and Freddie about an hour later. Once he arrived, he offered me more than enough money to pay for the room. I was not sure if he was being polite or showing me that he would pay for sex - if that was what I wanted. Since I did not want to send the wrong message, I took only enough money to pay for the room. What occurred was perfunctory sex. Perhaps Freddie was distracted because he stared at my breasts in admiration! After sleeping together, we went to dinner and agreed to meet again. That one night led to an almost 4-year affair!

At the culmination of my three months on the night shift, I requested an extension to remain on nights. Management denied it, as they were preparing for the Christmas mail volume. This meant that all employees were needed in their regular assignments so that staffing could support management's planning efforts. Consequently, I was required to return to evenings. Fortunately, the temporary change of schedule was positive for my daughter. Her behavior improved, and our relationship was much better.

Our second "date" was at his house. Our clandestine affair consisted of a rendezvous at least once, if not twice, a week. At some point, Freddie began working the day shift. So, depending on our schedules, he would sometimes come to my house, but we spent more time at his. Eventually, I adjusted to our superficial relationship, maybe even liked him a little.

At one point, Freddie asked me about my relationship with James, which was not surprising since it was such a tall tale. So, I gave him the Cliffs Notes version, concluding with the bogus proposal.

Freddie said, "He probably asks everybody to marry him!" Freddie even asked me what was going on between my lunch buddy and me. People at the post office had begun speculating that my lunch buddy and I were having an affair.

"Nothing," I answered, "We're just friends." *He had some nerve questioning me!*

Meanwhile, a year or so later, I could choose or "bid" (based on seniority) for my next assignment. I bid a customer service position, which meant I could work the day shift. The job required passing both a knowledge-based and memory exam. I passed both and became a full-time employee with a bona fide career with the Postal Service. The title of my customer service position was pool clerk. Pool clerks worked at multiple offices and filled weekly vacancies as needed. On my first day, my manager congratulated me on achieving 89 on the knowledge-based test. I also had an assigned supervisor named Rita. As a new pool clerk, I was scheduled to work with the on-the-job trainers for an extended period.

One night, I arrived at Freddie's house and one of his brothers had moved in temporarily. I noticed that his brother was checking me out. I did not think much of it until Freddie and I had gone into Freddie's bedroom, and Freddie hung back to speak with his brother. He closed the bedroom door, and he and his brother were on the other side, whispering. When Freddie came into the bedroom, he asked me if I was interested in having sex with two men. I told him, *no*. However, I thought he had lost his mind. *Did he really think I would agree to a ménage à trois?* But I was the idiot in the house with two men! Then I said, "Why did you ask me that?" The question went unanswered. I knew Freddie would not admit that his brother had made that request when they were outside the bedroom door whispering, and I was right.

I will never forget the night that Freddie realized I had a brain! Some evenings we would have small talk before retiring for another romp. We were watching music videos, which was one of my favorite pass times. Elton John's music video for the song "Nikita" was on TV, and I commented about the very stylish hat that Nikita was wearing. At some point, we discussed my receiving a full scholarship for college. Freddie looked genuinely surprised. I found it quite amusing. *It's not my fault that you never bothered to really talk to me.* After that night, I began helping Freddie with some of his applications for promotion.

Around the same time, the Postal Service began having career awareness conferences. One of the many objectives of these conferences was to create more diversity in the workplace. People of color did not occupy many of the supervisory and higher-level positions. Consequently, the Postal Service held many career awareness conferences to inform and educate employees regarding the many careers and detail assignments (temporary higher-level vacancies) available. I attended several of these conferences, particularly the one that Freddie attended with a date. His date was not someone I had seen before at the post office or elsewhere. I did not like that at all! It was the first time that I realized my feelings for Freddie were more than superficial. As I watched them together from the corner of my eye, I noticed his date tried to hold his hand. Freddie then pulled his hand away from hers because he could see that I was watching them. *Freddie cares?*

Sometime after the conference, I phoned Freddie to ask if I could spend the night with him. He told me that if I did, I would have to park across the street because his girlfriend sometimes rode by his house to check on him. I agreed to do it that night. But when I called on another night, and he asked me to park across the street again, I defiantly said, "That's alright."

But before I hung up the phone, he said, "Come on."

That night, I parked either in the driveway or in the garage. Freddie did not ask me to park across the street again.

One day, Freddie and I were at the post office near a rear breakroom. Out of nowhere, Freddie asked me, "Would you marry me? Would you?"

I was taken aback. My only response was to shrug my shoulders. Then I said, "I don't know."

Honestly, I did not. I thought that there was no way Freddie was the marrying kind. *Why do I keep receiving these lame proposals?* Later, while lying in bed next to him, I asked Freddie, "Why did you ask me that?"

He said, "Just something I was thinking about at the time."

I said, "Oh, okay." I never mentioned it again and neither did Freddie.

It seemed that our affair became more intense after that night because we saw each other more often. When Freddie would call my house after I retired for the night, Cookie would bring the phone to my room and whisper, while pointing to the phone, "It's Freddie."

After handing me the phone, I would say hello and hear, "Carolyn, where you working tomorrow?"

Once I answered, he would say, "Want to come over?"

"Okay." I answered.

Then I would jump up, gather my things, and drive 30 minutes north to spend the night with Freddie. This happened quite often.

There were some nights things did not happen that way. One night, I had agreed to drive to Freddie's house then changed my mind. When I called back to advise about my change of heart, someone I assumed was Freddie answered the phone. I said, "Freddie, I'm not coming."

The man on the other end of the phone said, "Hold on, you tell him."

What was that about? I was so glad I did not go see him that night. I later learned that Freddie talked about our "relationship" with his friends. A friend of mine, who worked at one of the offices I was frequently assigned approached me one day. She said, "I heard you see somebody." Surprised by her comment, she further explained that she was friends with one of Freddie's friends. I felt forced to admit that I would see Freddie. *What is going on?*

My relationship with Freddie was no longer this secret rendezvous that only we shared. He was telling his friends about us! Of course, I told my sister and close friends about Freddie, and they teased me often. My sister called him a derogatory term because of our strictly sexual relationship. One of my friends told me, "Freddie needs to break off some of his "manhood" and plant it so he can grow some more!"

Soon, things between Freddie and I became too complicated. Freddie invited me to his house one day, which was a request that was not unlike any other day that he asked me over. However, this day was different. I had not been at his house too long, nor did I hear anyone knock on the front door. I observed Freddie abruptly walk toward the front door and open it. I looked up to see this woman who worked on the night shift standing at the door. As she walked in, Freddie said, "Lina, why didn't you call?"

I immediately excused myself and walked into one of the bedrooms – not his. I am not sure what transpired between them, but when Freddie came into the room to retrieve me, he said, "Carolyn, come out here."

I told him, "I don't know her."

He said, "I'll introduce you."

It was then that I realized she was not leaving. I had no idea what excuse Freddie had given her for my being there. After the introductions, I decided it was best that I leave. Once we were outside, Freddie walked me to my car. Disappointed, I slowly entered my car and sat down. Then, I looked up at Freddie and asked, "Why do I have to leave? *You* invited me over here."

He responded, "I didn't know she was coming."

Freddie stood outside of my driver's side door, looking down at me through the window. He appeared to see the hurt and disappointment in my face because as I looked at him, his facial expression changed to display surprise and then deep concern for me. I slowly looked away from him, turning my head and starting my car. Then, I reluctantly departed his driveway.

I am not sure how many days passed that I did not speak with Freddie. But the night finally came when he called me again. Cookie brought me the phone, pointing to it, and whispering, "It's Freddie."

When I answered the phone, he asked me to come over. I said, "No!"

He responded, "Why?"

"Because you gave me your rear-end to kiss!" I snapped back.

He said, "No, I didn't!"

"Yes, you did!" I responded.

Freddie did not give up. He continued calling me for several nights, asking me to come over. I continued saying, "No."

Then one night, he added, "Please!"

I relented.

I was uncomfortable when I arrived at his house that night. It was clear that he was pleased that I had finally come to see him, but it was not the same for me. However, the sex was passionate! He held me tightly, genuinely showing affection as he hugged and caressed my body. Despite his enhanced performance, I wanted to pull away from him more than ever, emotionally. I did not sleep at all that night. I laid there, looking up at the ceiling, angry with myself for giving in. *Why did I come?* Something had changed within me. The thrill was gone.

At work, I received sideways glances. I thought Lina had told everyone, but it was probably those few people she did tell who told everyone. One morning, I walked into Lina's sister, Gina. The encounter was extremely awkward; especially since Gina was engaged to marry James by this time – despite my warning to her not to accept his proposal. Naturally, I eventually received a phone call from Deannie reporting how everyone was so shocked about Freddie and me. Deannie stated that James expressed his disbelief by saying, "Carolyn and Freddie??" Then referring to Lina, Deannie said, "That's Freddie's girlfriend!"

"Is anybody Freddie's girlfriend!?" I asked.

Sometime after the incident at Freddie's house, there was another postal dinner and dance. This time, I did make a dress for the event. The dress was a drop-waisted, black and fuchsia number with a black, hip level sash, and a black faux handkerchief in the simulated breast pocket. I accessorized it with black high-heeled pumps and black beaded dangling earrings. I looked attractive and happy to be there. Unfortunately, my excitement dissipated when I was seated at a table with some women I did not know, but who apparently knew me. I could only surmise by their awkward glances and whispering that they were talking about Freddie and me. Even though Freddie was not engaged or married, he should have been the one treated like he was wearing the scarlet letter A, not me.

At that time, I thought it ridiculous that I was the center of all the gossip. I was considered the side piece, even though Freddie was not really "attached" to anyone. Apparently, I was the only one that knew he was not attached. Realistically, there were other women in Freddie's life. I knew that. I had always known that. That was who Freddie was. Surely, I was not the reason Freddie was unattached, or was I? In my opinion, monogamy was just not his modus operandi.

I quickly grew tired of being ridiculed at the table. So, I left the table before the function was over. As I was walking in the lobby of the banquet area, I heard Freddie call my name. When I turned around, he was with a male friend. I waved at him and kept walking in the opposite direction.

Somehow, I survived the scandal and continued seeing Freddie, but it was no longer the same. I thought I could handle the late-night rendezvous that were once full of excitement and intrigue. But I was wrong. One day, I told Freddie that I did not want to continue our clandestine relationship and wanted more from him. His response?

"I can't do that right now."

"Okay," I said. Then I stopped seeing him, just like that!

Freddie tried several times to get me to change my mind about seeing him. It was by no means easy to resist his advances, but I remained steadfast in my decision. Parting ways was even easier since I worked at different offices and did not have to see Freddie at work. Eventually, he stopped asking.

A year or so later, I returned to working evenings. During that time on evenings, I earned a supervisory assignment (detail), which required me to work in an area that Freddie sometimes managed. He often allowed his personal feelings for me to interfere with his professional responsibilities. He gave me big attitude regarding some work tasks just to mess with me, even when there was nothing wrong with my supervision.

Eventually, I was promoted to supervisor. Freddie's career took a turn for the worse. It was alleged that he had friendships with one or more employees involved in some type of illegal drug activity. I did not believe it because in all the times that I had been to Freddie's home, I never witnessed any such activity. I believed he may have been guilty by association with the wrong crowd. Nevertheless, Freddie was suspended from work, pending investigation.

During Freddie's suspension, a mutual friend of ours advised me that Freddie was not doing well. I was tempted to visit Freddie, but I did not think it wise. I did not want to be a crutch for Freddie. I believed that if I helped him get through that bad time and then watched him return to doing what was natural or normal for him when things were better, he would just take me for granted – again! I felt relationships should form when people are at their best, which is where I believed Freddie and I were when we were seeing each other before. It appeared that Freddie was at his worst now and I did not want to get involved.

Then, our mutual friend approached me a second time. He said Freddie was depressed. After hearing that, I was really bothered about what was happening to Freddie. I knew I still had feelings for him. I believed that he only wanted my attention because whoever he was with (when I told him I wanted more from him) was no longer there. Since I did not want to be the second choice, I told our mutual friend, "Don't tell me anymore!" It was clear by the look on our mutual friend's face that he expected more from me regarding Freddie.

Nevertheless, he complied with my wishes and simply responded, "Okay."

I did not receive any further updates on Freddie from our friend or anyone else. Soon after, Freddie resigned or was terminated.

About eight years or so later, I saw our mutual friend again. When I asked about Freddie, he said Freddie had relocated to another state and was doing well. I asked for Freddie's phone number and eventually contacted him. I felt Freddie was pleased to hear from me. I told him that I would give him a call the next time I was in his city.

Freddie and I have managed to keep in touch over the years. He even got married! I told him, "She must be pretty special if he got married!"

He replied, "She alright!"

Freddie admitted that he did not run after women like he used to!

Instant Replay

The Womanizer

As you recall, I was a newbie regarding experiencing vomit. So, there I was, newly divorced, very much having greater expectations for a love relationship. When I met James, I was so excited to embark upon what I thought would be a normal, mature, and healthy relationship. Therefore, I was not using or even categorizing people and situations as vomit - yet. Albeit the charming and handsome vomit that James was! He was definitely the kind of man that you warn your daughters about.

When Stacy approached me, it was the first sign of acid reflux! I attempted to confirm with James that some two-timing was amiss. But not only did James avoid answering my question(s) about Stacy, he said she was dating Dave. Next, I told James a lie, thinking he would admit that he was not serious about getting married. Instead, he showed no objection to continuing the deceitful game he played with me and others, confirmed by Deannie, who was a useful resource, although not my friend. Finally, Divine intervention presented the revelation about the baby, just in time to prevent me from falling further into the abyss of James' unaccountable world!

Cookie was the objective eye I needed when the façade began to fade. Together, we could strategize, a skill I honed later and used many times personally and professionally. However, there were still times that vomit hid under the guise of deceit. Therefore, when I met Freddie, I was determined to play by my own rules, but my heart got in the way!

Ladies' Man

My relationship with Freddie was the vomit that chased me like "The Blob!" I bathed in it and loved its aroma. It was irresistible! I must admit that I was addicted to the sex! The sex was like a pharmaceutical drug prescribed to ease extreme pain that makes you feel so good. Just like drug abuse is not good, sex abuse is not good, especially in the absence of other vital relationship elements! However, it was great to have the sexual benefit of a relationship without the work that went along with it.

Initially, I was not interested in actively seeking a monogamous relationship. If it had happened, I would have welcomed it. But I had often watched other people's relationships begin and end, as well as my own. I *was* perfectly fine with my choices.

More than likely, Freddie would not have understood my plight as being perceived as a side piece, even though he was not engaged or married. A few years after my promotion, I assisted Lina and Gina with their applications for promotion. By this time, all of us had matured and understood relationships were either monogamous or not; analogous to a man being committed or not. In the case of Freddie, our professional goals superseded the personal drama we once shared.

Gina and I eventually worked in the same office, and continuously assisted each other with completing promotional applications and other sensitive documents until I retired from the Postal Service. Gina eventually told me she should have heeded my warning about James. I always liked Gina and felt compelled to tell her what I genuinely believed about James, hoping I could save her from heartache.

It was only after I was caught at Freddie's house, and subsequently hurt and disappointed, that I *recognized* the relationship as the vomit it was. Although I began to wean myself from Freddie, I never really allowed myself to heal. In hindsight, wanting a commitment with Freddie pushed me to start another relationship prematurely. It was the new relationship that set the example for what a total disregard of commitment and support were in a relationship, and the deceit that went along with it.

Consequently, I was forced to see the importance of those significant elements in a relationship – that realization will remain with me for the rest of my life!

> *[3] No one who hopes in you will ever be put to shame, but shame will come on those who are treacherous without cause. [4] Show me your ways, Lord, teach me your paths. [5] Guide me in your truth and teach me, for you are God my Savior, and my hope is in you all day long. (Psalm 25:3-5 NIV)*

Prayer:
Lord, sometimes we choose the people in our lives with the wrong motives, then we get what we get, and are disappointed. Father, teach us to choose better for ourselves, help us to know what and who we need in our lives. Lord, many times we are lonely, impatient to wait for the right person. Father, strengthen us so that our bodies are not weak; give us the wisdom not to accept whoever approaches us, and the ability to focus on what is inside of people and not their outside appearance. Lord, we will place our hopes and dreams in Your hands. Father, we love You and we praise Your holy name, in Jesus' name we pray, amen.

Part III – The Second Quarter
CHAPTER 4

Blocked!

Earlier I mentioned completing my on-the-job training (OJT) prior to beginning my pool clerk position. OJT was performed in the window services section of the post office, adjacent to the workroom floor. Even though it was a separate operation, it was located in the same building.

It was during this time that I met Michelle. Michelle had been on several higher-level detail assignments but not awarded a supervisory position yet. She was very smart and knowledgeable regarding the politics of the postal environment, especially on the workroom floor. She showed me where the bulletin board was located and encouraged me to monitor it often for job vacancies.

Michelle thought I had potential and the ability to do more at the Postal Service. She explained a process called PASS (a performance assessment) which used a rating system to identify and create a list of applicants for higher level assignments (details). PASS required the completion of an application comprised of several complex questions. I used my previous work experience to answer the questions. Once my application was reviewed, I received an above-average rating. I felt like I had won the lottery! Receiving an above average rating meant I was among the top applicants and could be considered for details in my local office.

Soon after, a co-worker told me she overheard someone discussing that I would replace the Express Mail coordinator/supervisor who was scheduled for maternity leave. Sure enough, Larry (the manager) summoned me. When I walked into Larry's office, it was evident by the look on his face that I was not who he expected to see. Afterall, he had chosen me based on a rating associated with my name on the PASS list and had no idea who I was or what I looked like. Despite his reaction, he gave me the detail.

I was detailed for approximately three months as the "acting" supervisor for the small Express Mail office. The Express Mail supervisor was scheduled to train me prior to her absence. Unfortunately, the training was cut short when she began her leave earlier than originally planned.

I supervised two employees. One received me graciously, while the other, named Sandy, did not. Sandy was incredibly angry that she had not been offered the detail. It was obvious that she harbored some resentment, demonstrated by her defiance whenever asked to do something in the office. If I asked Sandy a question about an office task or procedure, she was argumentative, and her explanations were always vague regarding the daily operations of the office. Sandy was an information hog! Her goal was to prove that she would have been the better choice. Sandy wanted me to fail.

I had several heated conversations with Sandy about her attitude. One day, the labor relations manager passed by our office and overheard the way Sandy spoke to me. He later told me to take control of the office and not allow her to behave in that manner. I had no idea how to address Sandy or the situation. However, I noticed that Sandy's attitude changed when she turned around from her desk one day (which was in front of mine), to look at me while I spoke with a customer on the phone. She was surprised that I could answer questions and speak intelligently to a customer. Sandy realized despite her efforts to thwart my progress, I had learned the processes of the office and she was no longer more knowledgeable than me!

Then I met Jen. The Express Mail office was used as a pass through by many managers and supervisors. Jen sashayed through the office one day and slowed her pace when she saw me. I had seen Jen many times before, but we had not met. She was a senior customer service representative – a coveted position because it allowed the use of a company vehicle and required little supervision. On that day we were finally acquainted. Jen seemed curious about how I obtained the detail assignment. Realizing her unasked question, I said, "You want to know how I got it."

She replied, "Yeah, how did you get it?"

Jen could not believe that I had actually "earned" the opportunity by successfully applying through the PASS process. We became fast friends. I would soon understand why my earning the detail opportunity was so unbelievable.

Once my three-month detail was over, I was smitten! I could not wait to apply for my first promotion. I returned to my pool clerk position and immediately began receiving assignments to fill weekly vacancies at several offices. I received my weekly assignments via interoffice mail the week prior from Rita. That was the extent of our interaction and communication.

When I applied for the first promotional opportunity, I found that the application required a supervisor's evaluation. Since Rita was my supervisor, I listed her on the application. I rarely saw Rita while on my detail, even though we were in the same building. I should have asked her for an evaluation before listing her on my application. Imagine my surprise to learn that Rita indicated on my application that I spoke "ungrammatically!" Fortunately, I had an ally in personnel who alerted me of this underhanded deed. I was angry, but I could not help but wonder why she wanted to sabotage me, marring my reputation and career before it even started! I had no idea why Rita did not like me. We barely had any conversations before my detail, and we only communicated through interoffice mail after my detail. Nevertheless, I did not confront Rita. But I ensured that she would not receive another application of mine!

I soon realized that the advantage of working in multiple offices allowed me to network with quite a few managers who liked me and admired my work ethic. By this time, I was even more encouraged and motivated to get a promotion. Therefore, I decided to be smarter regarding my applications and career goals. I asked the managers at the offices I worked most for permission to use them as references on my applications. When they agreed, I was able to circumvent Rita!

In the meantime, Jen decided to coach and prepare me for a pending vacancy in customer service. We met at a local library and Jen taught me everything I needed to know about the job to prepare me for the interview. When I applied for the position, I got an interview. Jen later told me that although I did not get the job, her manager was impressed with me. Sure enough, he called and offered me a detail in the main office, which was only 30 minutes from my home. I was excited and incredibly proud of myself.

The following day, I received another phone call from Jen's manager. He began the conversation with an apology and explained that Larry (the manager who gave me my first detail) would not release me. I was devastated and cried like a baby! I considered the career awareness conferences touting the detail opportunities that were equally available to everyone. So, I decided to simply ask Larry why he refused to release me.

When I approached Larry with my question, he responded that someone from our office was already working in the main office. I asked Larry how long she had been working there and he said a little over three months. I asked, "Why not bring her back and give me a chance?"

The look on Larry's face showed that he thought I was way out of line – he was so easy to read. I do not remember his reply, or even if he had one. But he did not change his mind about releasing me for the detail.

Determined, I wrote a formal letter to Larry, copying the postmaster, attempting to rally support for my release to perform the detail. In the letter, I challenged Larry to give me the opportunity based upon the organization's commitment to diversity and upward mobility. Nevertheless, Larry did not release me. I imagined him taking much pleasure in ignoring my letter. Upon speaking with the postmaster regarding Larry's decision, he nonchalantly said, "I don't know why Larry did that." I relented.

I continued applying for customer service positions in other areas and received quite a few interviews. I pursued this objective for about two years to no avail. I had hoped that some manager would have at least offered me a detail after all the applications I submitted and interviews I had received. It was then that I learned detail opportunities, most times, depended on *who you know*. I finally understood why Jen was in disbelief about my earning that first detail.

At this juncture, I decided that the competition and politics in customer service were too much for me to combat. I believed that if I returned to the workroom floor, where I first began my career, I would have more promotional opportunities. Consequently, I bid for an evening position on the workroom floor and formulated an alternative plan to be promoted.

"... [14] The Lord will fight for you; you need only to be still." (Exodus 14:14 NIV)

He's My What?

Early one morning, in 1987, I looked outside my bedroom window after hearing a loud engine coming from the front of my home. Although it was still dark, I could see an 18-wheeler, tractor trailer parked on the street. I was familiar with 18-wheelers because my father was a long-distance truck driver for True Value, formerly Food Fair/Pantry Pride. I watched as Danny emerged from the shadows of the truck to approach my bedroom window.

I had not seen Danny in two years, when my daughter was 4 years old. At that time, she had begun asking about her father. I imagine kids in her pre-school class were talking about their fathers. Danny had not taken any initiative to call me about her or visit. I was truly angry about his lack of compassion. I am not sure why I was surprised that he had not shown up. Although I had mixed feelings about my daughter seeing Danny, it was not about me or my feelings. It was all about her – for that reason, I took my daughter to see him.

Two years prior, Danny was easy to find because he lived in the same low-rate weekly motel establishment that his homeboy Willie lived with his girlfriend – yeah, they were still together. When I arrived, the three of them were outside as if waiting to greet us, and I had not forewarned Danny. It was quite interesting that they seemed to be expecting us. When I explained my reason for being there, they stared at us. I felt my child move closer to me as she held my hand tighter. *Baby, you ain't even got to worry 'bout me leaving you here!* The meeting did not play out as I expected because there was no meaningful conversation. It was unfortunate that Danny had nothing to say or offer her. *At least she knows he exists.*

Here it was, two years later, and he approached my bedroom window. *At least he has a decent job. Driving 18-wheelers pays well!* After we exchanged a few words through the window, he asked to come in and speak with me. Curious, I let him in. When he sat down, I could see him struggling with whatever was on his mind. Finally, he said, "I'm lonely."

As I listened, it took me a couple of minutes to understand what, or more specifically, *who* he was referring to. Then it clicked, "You're talking about me?"

He stared at me without providing a response, but he must have nodded his head or something that indicated I was correct, because I said, "It has been four years [since we divorced] and you have not even called to ask about our child. You think I want to get back with you?"

I am sure I said some other things, but the last thing I remember saying was, "... Besides, I don't love you anymore!"

It was blatantly obvious that my last statement was not what he expected to hear from me, because Danny left very quickly afterwards.

Several months later, Danny stopped by again. This time, my daughter was at home and my sister was visiting. I will never forget the look of confusion on my daughter's face as she stared at him. Her facial expression screamed, *he's my what?* My daughter had nothing for him – no conversation, no hello. Since Danny did not say much to her, what could she say to him?

Career Suicide

It was rather simple to get another job on the workroom floor because very few people left the day shift to return to the evening or night shift. Once I began working in my new assignment, I had to become reacclimated to the workroom floor because there had been several operational changes, mostly because of automation. There was a lot less manual mail processing happening. I also needed to develop a strategy to accomplish my goal of getting promoted!

Of course, I had second thoughts about giving up days so easily. Perhaps, if I had a permanent position at one of those customer service offices, I could have concentrated my promotional efforts at one of them. As it was, I was interviewing all over the place for higher-level positions. Even when I accomplished becoming one of the top three recommended for promotion, I would not get the position if another applicant, one who had also made it to the top three, had been pre-selected even before I was interviewed. Sometimes positions were posted just for show, adhering to a policy or procedure. Another thing that hindered me from being promoted was that some selecting officials were unfamiliar with me and my work ethic. As a pool clerk, I was not establishing real roots at any of the offices – not to mention that Rita was still my supervisor.

As I readjusted to the workroom floor, there was a meeting where five key managers, including one from personnel and one from finance, held a forum to discuss available detail and promotional opportunities within the Postal Service. It appeared to be an attempt to create more diversity in the workplace, and I was anxious to attend and hear what would be said. As I sat there observing their posturing, I recognized managers who I had met during my quest for detail and promotional opportunities while on days. It was just a dog and pony show! I could not sit idly by listening to untruths about their willingness to mentor and offer detail opportunities. So, I politely stood up and said, "I have spoken with most of you, with the exception of two, about available details and none of you have given me an opportunity."

I seriously wanted a chance to prove myself. I believed if they were sincere about wanting to help me or anyone else, I would have been given an opportunity. Later, one of the employees who also attended the forum said she could not believe that I had spoken up. I, on the other hand, knew I had committed career suicide. But I was not deterred.

Eventually, I approached Beverly, the manager of the evening shift, and told her my desire to become a supervisor. I asked her if she would consider me for a detail, if or when she had a vacancy. I do not remember her saying yes, but she did not say no. Soon, Beverly began observing me while I worked. I did not notice her at first, but one day I caught her watching me. Beverly had a "no nonsense" reputation. I realized she had probably been watching me for quite a while. I understood why she would not want to give me a detail or even promote me if I were lazy.

The day finally arrived that I was trained to supervise an operation of the workroom floor. Jim was the general supervisor for that area, and Beverly was his manager. I worked hard coordinating with Jim to ensure my assigned operation ran smoothly; and learned to control or eliminate downtime to the extent possible. Jim appeared to appreciate my efforts.

Finally, I applied for a supervisory position, but I no longer had the dependable and trustworthy application references I had gained from customer service. At this point, I only had Jim, my direct supervisor. Jim and I worked well together, and I believed he had no reason to evaluate me negatively. But, when I did not receive an interview, I became suspicious. I requested a copy of my final application from personnel. Once I read what Jim had written about me, I was furious! Strangely, Jim's comments on my application referenced an encounter I had with one of his friends who I had recently supervised. The friend had become upset when I did not approve his leave request. My decision was not personal and based only on the staffing needs of the operation. Why would Jim evaluate me based on that encounter, and not my work ethic? It was apparent that his friendships with the employees I supervised was stronger than his appreciation for my work.

Too angry, or stupid, to think of requesting a professional meeting, where two level-headed and mature people could discuss their differences, I confronted Jim right in the middle of the workroom floor! My actions created a scene, especially when I pointed my finger in his face! I reacted out of emotion and had not thought it through. I can still remember the look on Jim's face, flabbergasted that I approached him. I had committed career suicide – again, and at that moment, I did not care!

I desperately wanted to prevent Jim, or anyone else, from sabotaging my application efforts again. I went to Beverly and showed her what Jim had written about me. I told Beverly that Jim's evaluation was not based on my work at all. I explained to her what happened between me and the employee and how I believed that Jim and the employee were friends. I expressed my disappointment about Jim allowing his personal relationship with the employee to interfere with his professional judgment. After listening to my explanation, Beverly said she understood and allowed me to circumvent Jim by using her name instead for my future supervisory evaluations.

Just when I thought things were going quite well with Beverly, she discontinued my detail. I do not recall anything negative happening, but it could have been to simply give someone else an opportunity. One evening, things went awry in the operation that I had previously supervised. Apparently, whoever supervised the operation made a mess of things. Gigi, the night shift manager, was forced to staff the operation by taking employees from other operations, which caused downtime for those operations and the night shift. Gigi was not happy. As a result, Gigi asked Beverly to resume my detail. After that, I earned a good reputation on evenings and received several details to supervise in other operations.

Shortly thereafter, a supervisor vacancy was finally posted for the evening shift. I remember Beverly asked me if I had applied. When I said, *yes*; she responded, *good!* It was as simple as that. I was ready this time. I cannot recall if Beverly or another supervisor completed my evaluation for the application, but it was not Jim! While participating in the interview, I did not find the questions difficult at all. The interview panel was impressed with me as the answers rolled off my tongue. But what they did not know was that I had been there before. I had learned the answers to similar questions. I had also gained knowledge and experience working in the actual operations and not just textbook knowledge as was the case so many times before. I could relay actual scenarios of real-time issues that I had resolved while supervising on the workroom floor. I can only assume that I was recommended for promotion because in 1989, a little over a year after leaving customer service, Beverly promoted me!

[6] Surely you need guidance to wage war, and victory is won through many advisers. (Proverbs 24:6 NIV)

Instant Replay

Blocked

I had no issues getting interviews or jobs before I began my career with the Postal Service. My background, education, and eagerness to work was more than enough. There were no formal interviews required to work at the Postal Service. I passed a not-so-simple entry exam which required a passing score of at least 75%. However, there was an orientation which advised of the dos and don'ts and included a brief visit from a postal inspector. What was not emphasized were the other tests that would eventually be required to keep the job. Not to mention, the unwritten rules learned along the way regarding the application and interview processes, which too many times were not in my favor!

Recently, I enrolled in an online audit course entitled "Auditing Corporate Culture," to earn continuing professional education credits for my audit certification. The course explained the culture of some organizations. When I read quotes by Peter Drucker, father of post-war management thinking,

"Culture eats strategy for breakfast" and *"unhealthy culture can determine business strategy..."*

I thought, *oh my God, that is the Postal Service!* Unfortunately, I do not remember the course offering any textbook strategies or suggestions to combat corporate culture. However, a recap of the first half of my career will offer some real time advice.

Michelle was my first *star*. The Lord sent her to guide me to the bulletin board and encourage me to complete my first application for detail assignments. As an unknown individual, I was able to transcend biases and allow my above average evaluation to speak for itself.

Then Larry gave me my first detail opportunity. My initial interaction with Larry revealed that I would never have been his first choice for the detail. Unbeknownst to him, God had made the decision. When the Lord decides where he wants you to be, he places you in that position despite the Larry's of the world. He will also provide confirmation so that you know it was Him! I am certain that Larry would have reversed his decision to detail me, had he been able to do so without revealing his blatant bias towards me.

I was blindsided by Rita's implication that I was not well spoken. It was a boldfaced lie! She could not fathom my desire for growth. Was I supposed to be complacent in my pool clerk position? Did I not deserve a seat at the table? Obviously not. Apparently, I only deserved the scraps from that table!

When the Lord gifted me with my second *star,* Jen, she provided the necessary guidance to propel me to the next level. Jen prepared me for completing my first application for a specific job and coached me to become a competitive interviewee for that same job. Although I did not get that job, I was impressive enough to receive a second detail opportunity. However, despite Jen's and my efforts, Larry blocked me from taking advantage of the second detail – which *I* earned fairly.

I finally *recognized* that I was wallowing in the vomit of defeat remaining on the day shift and in customer service. I made the difficult decision to try an alternative path and *purged* the entire customer service experience. Upon returning to the workroom floor, I realized I had gained a new perspective of the Postal Service. I was a little wiser about the culture and *who-you-know* politics.

Career Suicide

Then the Lord gave me a third *star* for guidance, Beverly. I had to work harder for Beverly to recognize my worth. This time I had the courage to ask Beverly for exactly what I wanted. I likened my request to the specificity God wants us to have in our prayers. Although getting promoted was my unspoken prayer, God blessed me because of my commitment!

My previous experience with Rita should have prepared me for Jim, but I had yet to embrace the lesson. I still believed that my work ethic would be enough to warrant me a fair evaluation. But it was not just me, it was the culture – *"culture eats strategy for breakfast."* I had never addressed Rita for her conduct, but I confronted Jim thereby committing *career suicide*!

God defined my path by placing Gigi in it, even after Beverly intervened and controlled my supervisory evaluations. Gigi was an unexpected, yet necessary ally. Gigi's input brought my value as an effective supervisor to the forefront, encouraging Beverly to use my talents again and eventually promote me.

CHAPTER 5

The Bet

Approximately one year before being promoted to supervisor, I crossed paths with this guy while I was walking towards the break room. He was headed in the opposite direction, returning to the workroom floor. His first words to me were, "Would you like to cook me dinner?"

I said, "You can take me to dinner!

Obviously, that was a line and I fell for it!

At some point, we met again during a 15-minute break. When I asked his name, he replied, "Danny."

I uttered, "Hmph!"

He said, "Why'd you do that?"

I responded, "My ex-husband's name is Danny."

This Danny (Dan), however, had two very small diamonds, one each in his two front teeth. I decided not to hold his name or the jewelry in his mouth against him. But I should have.

Dan was very charming. I shortened his name to distinguish him from the first Danny in my life. I learned he had a young daughter. Not sure why I did not think about the possible baby mama drama that might accompany his daughter. However, we were always hanging out, either at dinner or dancing. One night his baby mama was at the night club too! It was not even a local night club – it was down south, at least an hour and a half from where she lived. Nevertheless, she confronted Dan while we were on the dance floor, saying, "What are you doing having fun while your baby needs milk!" The confrontation dampened Dan's spirits and we left the club.

When Dan and I finally had sex for the first time, I experienced my first orgasm. It was indescribable! I did not know what was happening to me. None of my girlfriends had ever discussed orgasms with me, so I had not realized I was missing something during sexual intercourse. Then I remembered when Freddie told me he was unable to give me an orgasm. Unintentionally stroking his ego, I told him I had had one. I really thought that feeling of excitement and becoming moist during sex was evidence of an orgasm. I was *so* wrong!

I cannot even begin to explain why sex was even tolerable up until that point. *How had I found pleasure in sex without having an orgasm? What was I really feeling during sex that encouraged me to continue having sex?* It took me almost 10 years after having sex for the very first time to experience an orgasm. I sufficed it to say that maybe I had had an orgasm before, and it was just not a vibrant one! But whatever the reason *was*, I was having *vibrant orgasms* all the time with Dan! Unfortunately, I would learn that was the only mature thing that Dan was able to do for me.

Dan and I were always actively doing something new together. One weekend, we went on a cruise with alumni from my high school for a class reunion. Another weekend, we drove to Key West. It was the relationship that helped me forget about Freddie. A friend of mine named Pat cautioned me about getting involved with Dan because she said I was not over Freddie. But I disagreed with her and allowed myself to get deeper into a relationship with Dan.

Dan was charming like a snake and wooed me from the very beginning! He never asked me if he could move in with me, he just never went home. (Cookie had moved out a year prior and married.) It was easy to get sucked in because he was very nice to me. Each time he got paid, he contributed to my household, giving me enough money to cover my entire mortgage! He also bought me expensive gifts. However, Dan's first omission was the reason for his nightly peppermint breath. I did not learn that it was because he smoked marijuana until after I had fallen for him. I am sure that was intentional.

Dan's motive for our relationship was also another lie that I was too slow to learn. By the time I caught up to the game Dan was playing, I had fallen in love with him. Dan told me during a braggadocio moment that he and a male co-worker had made a bet that he could not "date" me. I am sure they did not use the word date. Once I learned this important fact, all that Dan represented himself to be became questionable. That is when I should have run.

Laying Pipes

One night I was leaving the post office and a woman was waiting for me by my car. I assumed it was his baby's mama. She told me Dan and she were still dating. I did not see how that could be possible since he was always at my house. Therefore, I did not believe her. When I questioned Dan, he acted as if she was a fatal attraction and denied seeing us both at the same time.

On one afternoon, after spending the night at my house, Dan was leaving for work. When I heard the front door open again, he returned to say that his car's window had been smashed. When I went outside to see what had happened, I observed that his car's rear window was indeed smashed. It appeared that someone had smashed it – a lot! We surmised that his baby's mama must have followed him to my house and busted the car's window! *Thank God it wasn't my car!*

I was unsure of what to do with Dan being dumbfounded, so I called the police. When the officers arrived, they laughed and said Dan was "laying pipes." I did not think it was funny, but the men sure did! Dan maintained that he was not doing anything to make his baby's mama smash the car's window. He claimed that she was just mad because he was not with her.

I was suspicious, but since Dan never went home, I could not figure out when he would have time to have another relationship. However, Dan never ever going home had its drawbacks. Once I found that he had violated my privacy by going through my things. Dan found a letter that I had written venting about Freddie, and he appeared to be jealous. On another day, when Dan would have normally given me his monthly contribution to my household, he decided not to. When I asked him about it, Dan asked me in a tone that indicated he thought he was *all that*, "What were you doing before I got here?"

I retorted, "If you don't want to contribute to *this* household, stay home!"

Consequently, Dan continued his monthly monetary contribution. Although it was great to have extra money, I did not need it. I certainly was not going to let Dan continue using the comforts of my home without paying for it.

Hot Mess!

The day I decided to introduce Dan to my daughter was during 1989 when we picked her up from school. She was about 7 years old at the time. When my daughter got into the car, Dan noticed that her eyes were hazel and asked if she were wearing contact lenses. I am sure he was attempting to be funny, but it was very silly of him.

One evening, Dan arrived at my house with ice cream, but he only brought enough ice cream for me. I thought that it could have been an unintentional omission because my daughter often stayed with my parents when Dan visited. However, when I asked Dan about it that very moment, he replied, "She doesn't have to get something every time I bring you something!"

My feelings were hurt because I believed my daughter's feelings were hurt. I later explained to Dan how selfish he appeared and that he was wrong, but I did not feel my point was received very well. However, I kept a mental note about the incident.

Our first major disagreement indirectly involved his 2-year-old daughter. It was a night unlike any other that Dan would come over after work. I was dressed in a sexy nightie, awaiting Dan like I had several nights before. As I heard him enter the front door, I laid on my bed expectantly. But when he came into my bedroom, he was carrying his toddler daughter. Dan proceeded to prepare the sofa in my room as a makeshift bed. I was taken aback because we had not discussed this visit. Therefore, I was not happy about what I was seeing. If I had been expecting them, I would not have been half naked when they arrived! Not to mention that I was still salty about his lack of compassion for *my* daughter.

I continuously accepted whatever story Dan told about the drama between him and his baby's mama. So, as I observed him make the bed for his daughter and not part his lips to say anything to me – almost like I was not even there, I felt disrespected. Afterall, it was my house. The least Dan could have done was prepared me by simply asking to bring his daughter to my house. One could think that he just wanted me to become acquainted with his daughter, and that I should have been okay with it. However, I knew that was not his intention. Dan expected more from me than he was willing to give.

When I questioned Dan about bringing his daughter to my house, he became terribly angry. I tried to explain that it was not about his daughter, but about him and the level of respect that I wanted or expected from him. Dan picked up his daughter and proceeded to leave. I tried again to explain that it was not about his daughter, which based on the foul language coming out of his mouth, he did not believe me. As Dan carried his daughter in his arms, holding her with both hands, he walked towards the front door. I reached out to him with my right hand, attempting to stop him from leaving and hoping to get him to listen to me. But instead, he bit me on my right forearm. I snatched my arm away and backed up in shock, watching him walk out the door. Yes, I had a small bite shaped bruise on my forearm and at least one small puncture wound. Although it was not deep, the skin was broken.

After Dan left, I called a friend and told her what happened. She came over to comfort me and suggested that I call the police. I really thought it was just a huge misunderstanding and that perhaps Dan believed I was exhibiting some aggression towards him and his daughter. For this reason, I did not call the police.

A day or so later, I went to the doctor. When asked what happened to my arm, I reluctantly admitted it was a human bite. The male nurse looked at me incredulously. I received a tetanus shot on that day. Honestly, I was more concerned about clearing up what I thought was a misunderstanding regarding his daughter than about the actual bite. Can you imagine that I wanted to fix that too? I did not want Dan thinking that I had an issue with his baby.

I do not recall if Dan ever apologized for biting me because he was always apologizing for something. Great sex was always included with his apologies. But instead of breaking up with Dan, I continued trying to make things work with him and what a hot mess it was!

Baby Mama

The very next visit to his parents' house confirmed that Dan had told his entire family that I did not want his baby at my house. As usual, Dan was outside with his brothers. My daughter and I were inside with his mother in the small sitting room. Soon after we arrived, entering the sitting room, one by one, were Dan's baby's mama and his two sisters. I became suspicious as I observed them each enter the room.

His baby's mama began speaking and said, "Why didn't you want my baby at your house when I *let* her come?"

The unmitigated gall! "The next time you want to *let* somebody to come to *my house,* ask me first!" I stood up and added, "Excuse me!" I grabbed my daughter by her hand, and we left.

I was so angry! The only thing that kept me from expressing myself with expletives was that Dan's mother was sitting there – who said absolutely nothing. Once I was in my car, my anger triggered tears to roll down my face. *The nerve of them thinking they could intimidate me! They actually tried to triple team me in front of my child!* Somehow, I ended up at Cookie's house. By that time, I was crying uncontrollably.

Cookie said, "You are crying because you didn't say what you wanted to say." All I could think about was how they were accusing me of having something against a baby, when his baby had nothing to do with it!

When I finally returned to my house, Dan was waiting for me. He apologized for what had transpired at his mother's house and reassured me that it would not happen again. However, it was not over for me!

CHAPTER 6

"Condition"

In 1991, four years after the last time I saw Danny, I ran into him at the A&W Root Beer drive-up restaurant in Miami. I was still sad because Danny had ignored our child. I spoke to him very sternly when he approached the driver's side of my car. Referring to the passenger side of my car, I said, "Go over there and speak to her!" Afterwards, he appeared to be ashamed. I made him feel guilty because soon after, he called to schedule a visit with my daughter.

When the time arrived for Danny to visit my daughter, he phoned and asked me if he could see her at my parents' house instead. "Why?" I asked.

He responded, "I don't want you to be there."

I had no understanding of the reasons behind this request. Nonetheless, I called my parents and asked them if it was okay that Danny visit my child at their home. My parents agreed. However, when I spoke with my 10-year-old daughter about the arrangement, she stated, "I want you to be there."

I tried to convince her that she would be fine with her grandparents present, but she insisted that I be there with her. In retrospect, it made perfect sense that she felt as she did.

I called Danny and explained my daughter was not comfortable with him visiting her at my parents' house. I again invited him to visit her at our home. But he was adamant about my not being present. So, a visit never happened, nor did Danny ever provide an explanation for this "condition."

Engaged?

Dan and I continued our relationship for two more years. We still had disagreements. Sometimes our disagreements became heated arguments and he always reverted to using foul language and name calling. I demonstrated my best use of profanity while with him. Whenever he pushed me, I pushed back! I blamed myself for allowing a cohabitation relationship to develop without discussing any rules or establishing personal boundaries. I should have also clearly defined what he could and could not do at *my* house. I attempted to rectify all of this too!

My efforts appeared to be successful because our communication improved, and we fought less. The relationship, outside of sex, seemed to be worth saving. *Why, you ask?* Dan was actually very funny. He was also an excellent poet and a pretty good artist. He wrote so many love poems while we were together that he had to make a notebook. Dan told me once that if he ever sold the poems to a record label, he would have to share the profits with me because I inspired him to write. Dan also drew my high school's mascot for the cover of my 10-year reunion program booklet. For a while, Dan's good qualities competed successfully with the bad!

Dan proposed to me at one of my most favorite places – the beach. We had previously attended a bridal show and picked out several engagement rings. The one with a baguette diamond setting was my favorite, and the one he ordered. Dan purchased the center diamond separately and it weighed a little over half a carat. The clarity was exquisite! Eventually, we began planning for our wedding and contracted to build a new home. By this time, my daughter and his daughter were approximately 11 and 4 years old, respectively.

CHAPTER 7

Fresh Start

In early 1992, I made a firm decision to return to college and complete my bachelor's degree. I had been attending college classes throughout the years but had not really made the commitment to finish any degree-seeking program. I learned about a program at Barry University that targeted working adults. It was not exactly conducive to my work schedule, but I split my two days off and attended some of the necessary classes. Surprisingly, my supervisors worked with me to manipulate my schedule, which accommodated attending classes. By the grace of God, it worked!

In the latter part of 1992, I transferred to a new office, anxious to get a fresh start for personal and professional reasons. By this time, my relationship with Dan had undergone at least two break-ups. Despite our being engaged, I no longer wanted to be in the same facility with him. I thought that transferring to a new office would provide the fresh start I needed to make new connections and references. However, Jim (my supervisor) transferred to the new office too! He was promoted to the manager of the evening shift, which meant he was no longer my direct supervisor, but I was still one of his subordinate employees.

Frozen Feet!

Dan began acting strangely approximately one month before our wedding which was planned for December 1992. I did not want to believe that after being with Dan for almost five years that he was backing out – but he did, and the invitations were already mailed. He not only had cold feet, but frozen feet! I was so ashamed and embarrassed to personally notify my guests and wedding party. Therefore, one of my dearest friends notified everyone for me. Much later, my mother told me that my father cried. I can only imagine how much he hurt for me.

I struggled to maintain the façade that I was okay. My immediate family was ecstatic that the wedding was off, but no one told me! Perhaps if someone had said something to me, it may have helped me to heal and become stronger. I attempted to move on with my life without Dan and had even begun dating again. However, Dan did not want to see me move on without him or with anyone else. First, he wanted me to continue dating him like nothing had happened. When I refused, he consistently begged me to elope. Wrought with emotion, I did.

Afterwards, my parents were disappointed with my decision. My mother told me I was stupid. She eventually apologized to me and said that the Spirit of the Lord told her He was in control of all things. It was not until later that I realized Dan only convinced me to elope because he knew my parents would have intervened and convinced me not to marry him if they had known.

To make matters worse, when I told my 11-year-old daughter that I had married Dan, tears came to her eyes. When I asked her why she was crying, she did not respond. I believed she simply did not want me to get married and that perhaps it was normal since it had only been she and I for such a long time. But her tears alone should have told me that she just did not want me to marry *Dan!*

Prayer:
Heavenly Father, we come to You for continued guidance when we are ashamed because of interactions with certain people and the decisions that we make. Lord, we know that You can fill the voids in our lives with undying love and support. Father, please remove the shame that we feel because we are impatient and accept the fake before waiting for what is real. Father, help us to remove the physical, emotional, and psychological attachments, so that we can see people for who they really are. Lord, help us to understand that it is because of Your intervention that we will be renewed, refreshed, and ready to receive Your continuous down-pouring of love and blessings upon our lives. Father, we love You and we praise Your holy name, in Jesus' name we pray, amen.

CHAPTER 8

Newlywed

As newlyweds, Dan and I attended a dinner party held at his family's place. It was the first outing since we had been married. Dan's older sister began talking about me, and I could hear her perfectly. She told a cousin that I *made* Dan get married. The cousin responded, "You can't make someone get married!" My feelings were extremely hurt.

Overhearing the conversation forced me to accept that marrying Dan was not going to change him. After all the begging he performed to convince me to elope, how could it be construed as making him get married. He had to have told his family that I *made* him get married. Where else would they get that from?

Dan's upbringing and family background was a negative influence on our marriage. Initially, it appeared that he tried to be a good husband, but Dan could only act for so long. We had moved into our new home and things were okay for a while. Dan even said, *I'm so happy!* But he soon reverted to the same person he was while we were dating. I felt stuck and disappointed that I exposed me and my daughter to him. Dan was not taught how to have a healthy love relationship. Therefore, he could not live it. I had married him, and as a result, I continued to try to improve our relationship.

After we had been married for a few more months, I convinced Dan to apply for an entry level position as a custodian. He was very good with his hands and a custodian position was the alternative path to becoming an electronic technician (ET). I attempted to encourage Dan to take an ET course at the local college. I thought I was successful when he finally registered for the course, but a few days later, he dropped the course and received a full refund. Since Dan had earned veteran preference after spending three years in the army, if he became a custodian, he could apply for an ET position and receive training. But Dan's pride prevented him from applying for a custodian position at his then current facility because he did not want to be seen by co-workers sweeping the floors. So, Dan applied for a custodian position at my facility.

Soon after Dan submitted his application, I was approached by the maintenance manager at my facility. He was the deciding official for the custodian position. He explained to me that he wanted to hire Dan because he was my husband, but since Dan's attendance was atrocious, he could not. I stood there in disbelief because I was unaware that Dan had an attendance problem. The supervisor offered to show me Dan's attendance record, but I declined. I knew that if Dan believed his privacy was violated, and with my not being his "official" supervisor, he would have filed a grievance against me and the maintenance manager. It would have been an opportunity for Dan to divert attention from the real issue of his not reporting to work.

At my first chance to speak with Dan, I told him about my conversation with the maintenance manager. I assured Dan that I had not seen his attendance record. I concluded with asking him, "Where exactly are you going each day when you leave home pretending to go to work?" All the while thinking, *You idiot!* Of course, that question was not answered.

Also, during our first year of marriage, Dan and I had an extremely loud argument, so loud that our neighbor (who was also a police officer) called the police. The argument began because I reminded Dan that garbage day was on the following day. I may have said something as simple as, "Don't forget to take out the garbage tomorrow." My tone was not condescending, mean, or nasty, but it set him off and an argument ensued. My daughter was at home this evening. She was around twelve years old by this time. I yelled towards her bedroom consistently and repeated during the argument, "I'm okay!"

When the police arrived, Dan answered the door. They asked to see me, and Dan called my name. I had retreated to my daughter's room. Once I showed myself without lumps or bruises, the police asked me a couple of questions. Satisfied with my answers, they left. Once they were gone, I told Dan that if he argued with me in that way again, he would be going to jail. Surprisingly, that was the first and last time that he behaved in that manner. Unfortunately, Dan transitioned into becoming more verbally and psychologically abusive.

During another disagreement, Dan screamed directly into my ear. It was loud and extremely uncomfortable. It was intangible torture. I also observed him alienate my daughter by making her feel as if she and I were not a package deal. In response to my telling him about the latter behavior and his lack of parenting skills, he told me, "She'll be gone (to college) soon," as if it excused him from expending any effort to develop or repair their relationship. However, I never allowed his inability to be a loving stepfather to my daughter to influence or change my behavior and ability to be a loving stepmother to his daughter.

[7] Whoever corrects a mocker invites insults; whoever rebukes the wicked incurs abuse. (Proverbs 9:7 NIV)

Me too!

I also experienced sexual harassment during the early years of my marriage. It was during the time when Jim was my manager. The Postal Service hired many transitional employees (TEs) to help with seasonal volumes of mail. There was one TE named Earl whom I will never forget. He was a young, clean-cut, pleasant guy who worked well in any operation that he was assigned.

On a Saturday in 1994, Earl approached me saying matter-of-factly (and I paraphrase), "Tommy told me to tell you he wants to have sex with you."

"Excuse me?" I replied.

Earl repeated, "Tommy told me to tell you he wants to have sex with you."

Stunned, I stood there in disbelief about what I had heard. Then Earl said, "Is something wrong?"

I responded, "No," not wanting to get Earl any more involved than he was already. I had to think about the implications of what he had just said to me.

Another supervisor, who apparently observed my exchange with Earl, walked over to me and asked, "Are you okay?"

The question must have been the direct result of the look of disgust and shock on my face. I repeated to the supervisor what Earl had said to me. She said, "What are you going to do about it?"

I responded, "I don't know!"

Tommy was another supervisor with whom I communicated almost daily about work. We coordinated regarding the operations we each supervised. Tommy seemed to be well liked by most employees and supervisors. He had a big afro and always wore the same kind of shirt with his slacks. Our conversations were always friendly. However, I had no idea that Tommy would send me such a message!

Tommy had propositioned me in the most insensitive manner. Not to mention we were both married. It was extremely unprofessional to put an employee in the middle of what should have been two-way communication between Tommy and me. Although, it was not a professional request or statement, I would have preferred that Tommy asked me directly. If he had, I could have responded to him that I was not interested and no one else would have known about it. As it was, Tommy put me and Earl in a very awkward position. What was he thinking? Did that really work with women?

Once I collected myself, I reported the incident verbally to Acting Manager Dave in Jim's absence. I got Joe involved on that same day. Joe was the president of the supervisors' union. It was unusual to have two supervisors at odds with one another. Joe dealt primarily with differences between supervisors and upper-level management. Nevertheless, Dave and Joe interviewed Earl. Earl admitted to saying exactly what I reported. Joe later told me that Earl thought it was a private joke between Tommy and me. I responded, "Are you kidding me?"

On Sunday, as if the day before was not bad enough, Tommy approached me while I was in my operation and began picking non-existent lint from my clothing. Furious, I immediately reported a second incident to Dave, and recapped both events in writing.

When Jim returned to work, I followed up to ensure both incidents were reported to him. He seemed indifferent. But, by this time, everyone had heard about what happened between Tommy and me. Dave was offended because he asked if I thought he had not handled the matter properly. I was not sure if he handled the matter properly or not. But either Tommy did not take the matter seriously because it was not handled properly the first time; or he did take the matter seriously and tried to cover his actions on Saturday by approaching me cavalierly and touching my clothing on the following Sunday. I surmised that because his message on Saturday was not received by me as he intended, Tommy hoped to down-play his actions on Sunday. This would have given the impression to anyone who may have been watching us that he and I were "familiar." Why else would he approach me a second time?

At least one manager and several employees asked me questions about what had transpired between Tommy and me. Each seemed to have an opinion regarding what I should or should not have done. Manager Carly told me that she would have spoken with Tommy directly. I disagreed with Carly and told her Tommy should have spoken to me directly and not have used an employee to deliver his message. If Tommy had spoken to me, my responding, *no* or *not interested* would have been a simpler resolution than my having to report the incident.

When another employee, who was also the union steward for the employees, approached me, she asked if I wanted Tommy to lose his job. I said, "If I wanted Tommy to lose his job, I would have filed a sexual harassment complaint." I further explained that my purpose was to simply let Tommy know that he was wrong; and the best way to do that without jeopardizing his job was to report the incident to Dave and Jim. I knew that it was important that I addressed the situation openly or it would have appeared that I condoned Tommy's behavior. I hoped that my actions taught Tommy a lesson. I felt ostracized because I was treated like the aggressor instead of the victim. Why did I have to defend my actions?

It was obvious that Jim felt a certain way about my reporting Tommy's sexual harassment. He did not address the situation with any sense of urgency, it was just not a big deal to him. Maybe it was common for men (in that atmosphere) to communicate their desire for women *jokingly*. Afterall, Earl thought it was a personal joke.

Eventually things calmed down at work and I imagined the union steward told Tommy that my intentions were not to cause him harm. Sometime later, there was a Black History event that included dinner and dancing. Tommy and his wife attended. Tommy asked me to dance with him on an up-beat tune and I did. I was curious as to why his wife did not dance with him. I always believed Tommy's pride prevented him from apologizing to me. In retrospect, his asking me to dance was his way of extending an olive branch. Me, on the other hand, danced with him to show that I had forgiven him for being stupid; and I had.

Instant Replay

Me Too!

Several years later, around 1997, I ran into Tommy at a local gas station. As I was putting gas in my car, Tommy pulled up behind me on a motorcycle. I had long since put our incident behind me, and by that time, I am sure Tommy had already retired from the Postal Service. He was very pleasant, and we exchanged small talk. Shortly thereafter, I learned that Tommy was killed in a motorcycle accident. I was saddened but pleased that we made peace with each other.

CHAPTER 9

Postal Inspector Application

One day, Jim complimented me out of nowhere. "You are really doing a good job with them," referring to one of the most difficult teams of employees to supervise. Although it felt good that Jim finally recognized me for my hard work, I was not convinced that he really appreciated me. I believed that if given another opportunity, he would stab me in the back again and not evaluate me fairly.

In late 1993, I noticed a recruitment poster for the US Postal Inspection Service, the only law enforcement branch for the Postal Service at that time. The Inspection Service was recruiting potential postal inspectors. The position required a bachelor's degree and at least two years of postal supervisory experience or a law enforcement background. I knew nothing about law enforcement, but that did not discourage me. Since I had been supervising for four years, I was ready for something different. Ironically, I only had one more month remaining before completing my bachelor's degree. Certain that I would be finished in time to meet the eligibility requirements, I submitted my application.

The application process for postal inspector was a long one. I knew that at some point, I would need an evaluation from my supervisor. My immediate supervisor's name was Cindy and I explained to her what had occurred between Jim and I several years prior. I told her I was positive he would sabotage me again if given another opportunity. Cindy agreed to keep my application process a secret and I listed her as my immediate supervisor on the application – and this time, she really was!

In 1994, just shy of two years at the new office, the Postal Service underwent a reorganization which included downsizing. Many supervisors were forced to relocate to other offices within and outside of my state because their jobs were eliminated. The managers had a meeting to determine who they would keep and who they would force to relocate.

Jim decided to choose someone else over me and I was *almost forced* to relocate. Carly, the manager of the day shift, who I had never worked for, chose me for her team of supervisors. When Carly discussed with me what happened at the meeting, she said, "Jim has a hard-on for you, girl!" I chuckled, explaining that it did not help things between Jim and I when I lost control some years prior during a conversation with Jim in the middle of the workroom floor! Carly explained that she wanted to prevent undue hardship on my young marriage. I thanked Carly for giving me a chance. To clear any doubt that Carly may have had regarding her decision to choose me, I assured her that I would continue to work hard. I also informed her about my pending application for postal inspector.

Have a Baby?

Once I applied for the position of postal inspector, I began changing my eating habits and teaching myself to run. I started running one residential block at a time, gradually adding another until I was running at least three miles. I also joined a local gym where the owner often gave individual training sessions. Eventually, I gained muscle and burned a great deal of fat. I even noticed some definition in my fat thighs!

It was during this time that Dan suggested we have a baby. He said we could afford it. I thought he must have lost his mind! But it was obvious that it was a ploy to interfere with my application process. However, I did not address my suspicions regarding Dan's request. I sternly told him that because of my application process, I was not having a baby!

Besides, I knew that our marriage was not strong enough to have a baby. I believed the only reason we were still together was because I worked days and he worked evenings. This simple fact limited the amount of quality time we spent together. I often thought about the seriousness of this fact. Although we shared Tuesdays and Wednesdays off each week, I knew those two days per week were not enough to infuse the marriage with qualities that were never there in the first place. I repeatedly told Dan that a marriage was more than just sex. I did not know what qualities I needed in a husband exactly, until they were not in mine. Dan seemed to think sex was the remedy for everything.

Instant Replay

Dan

The emotional attachment that I experienced with Dan was difficult to understand and even harder to explain. In hindsight, the relationship was the most tumultuous I had ever had. It was emotionally attaching and draining from the very first orgasm! Instead of terminating the relationship altogether, I remained just because I did not want to start over.

I realized that by allowing Dan to freely come to my house, he crossed personal boundaries that appeared unimportant at first until he began to take advantage of me and my kindness. His psychological abusiveness appeared second nature to him. I am not sure if Dan was even aware that his behavior was the textbook definition of psychological abuse.

> *Psychological abuse is defined as signs and symptoms which may "start small at first as the abuser 'tests the waters' to see what the other person will accept, but before long the psychological abuse builds into something that can be frightening and threatening."*

Psychological abuse is not one that is often discussed and when I learned the specific signs and symptoms:

> *"name calling, insulting the person, threatening the person or threatening to take away something that is important to them, imitating or mocking the person, swearing at them,*

ignoring, isolating the person, and excluding them from meaningful events or activities" (www.healthyplace.com).

Upon reading, I realized just how much I had been subjected to these behaviors during my relationship with Dan.

He was skillful in the art of love making and to my own detriment, I mistook that for love. It was that skill that Dan perfected and used as manipulation. It was also why he so confidently made and won that bet! However, it was that same skill that became so unimportant when he failed at being a descent husband and stepfather, coupled with the other absent elements of the relationship. The chain of events certainly gave me several chances to terminate the relationship with Dan. But that termination would not come soon enough!

CHAPTER 10

The Three Sisters

Dan came home late quite often. After learning about his attendance issues, the excuses he gave me for being late became even more questionable. If I awoke and he was not at home, I would call for him at his parents' home. Several times, his father told me he was not there. When I questioned Dan later, he would claim he was there. Once I asked him, "So are you saying your father is lying to me?" Dan had no response for me that night!

One night, I was asleep when he came home late. I awoke to observe him sitting at the foot of the bed, wringing his hands. He looked nervous and somewhat distressed. I asked, "What's wrong?"

Dan told me that he was in the parking lot at work and a woman approached him claiming to have shot herself in one of her breasts with her own gun. Dan said she asked for his help getting to the nearest hospital and he drove her there.

Since Dan and I both worked in the same facility before I transferred, I knew quite a few people who worked in his facility, including the woman who had been shot. She was one of three sisters, and I was acquainted with each of them. One of the sisters, Jo, and I had previously been friends. Another sister, Sue, worked in my facility. Betty is the sister who allegedly shot herself.

On the day following the shooting incident, I attended a meeting at my facility and my colleagues were discussing what happened at the other facility, which I believed at the time confirmed Dan's account of what had transpired the previous night. As I departed the meeting, I literally walked into Sue, who was surprised when I inquired about Betty's condition. I smiled and said, "My husband took her to the hospital." Sue responded with, "Oh, oh, she alright." Her reaction puzzled me because I expected some sort of gratitude or appreciation for my husband's manly deed. Something was *off*, but I just could not put my finger on it!

Mini Me

Sometime in 1995, I tried to encourage a second reconciliation between my daughter and Danny. At 14 years old, I believed it important that my daughter know Danny. I contacted him, explaining that since our daughter was older, he needed to get to know her. In response, we were invited to meet Danny and his new wife at their home. Upon meeting his wife, I noticed that although she was about 10 years younger than me, her personality was very similar to mine. It was like meeting my younger self!

During one of our few conversations, Danny admitted to me that his friends told him, "Man, you can't marry Carolyn twice!"

I told Danny that I recognized that his wife's personality was like mine. Danny said, "You weren't supposed to see that!"

Danny later planned two or three outings with my daughter. He did show up for at least one. But when he did not show for the last scheduled outing, my daughter was extremely disappointed. As a result of Danny disappointing my daughter, I scheduled an appointment with a child psychologist. I did not want my child to suffer any depression or anxiety because of her father's ignorance. The psychologist later told me that my child felt some resentment about my contacting Danny. I felt badly because my intention was to fill what I thought was a void, not create one.

I Did It!

The postal inspector application process had continued to progress. Cindy had already completed her supervisory evaluation of me, and Jim was none the wiser. I had also passed the entrance exam and a background check.

The last step in the application process was an assessment center evaluation. It encompassed a full day filled with individual and group exercises which were observed by several managers. I was so focused, interacting with my group, when necessary, that I forgot I was being monitored. When I returned home that evening, I was mentally and physically exhausted. It felt like forever while I waited for my assessment center results to arrive in the mail. When the results arrived only a few days later, it was exhilarating when I read that I had passed!

Then one day in 1996, when I was not at work, several postal inspectors descended upon the workroom floor and interviewed random employees about me. To my knowledge, Jim was not one of them. It appeared that the feedback from the employee interviews was positive because soon after, I was scheduled for an interview. The interview was the final step before being offered a position, and I was ready! Afterall, I had so much practice. My quest for promotion years prior prepared me for this moment. I was half-way there to begin what I *thought* would be the most important chapter of my life and career, but I was wrong!

Instant Replay

I Did it!

Larry, Rita, and Jim were the *vomit* that fueled my strategies and enabled me to prepare myself for what would come later in my career. Even the "M*e Too!*" moment introduced another part of the corporate culture in which I was immersed. I *managed* my Jim vomit when the Lord gave me Cindy who knowingly executed my plan to keep my postal inspector application process a secret. The Lord *managed* my Jim vomit (again) when Carly stepped in and saved me from being forced to relocate to another office or state. The totality of these circumstances and experiences helped me *survive* and *thrive* among a corporate culture that I was oblivious to. But I was only half-way there!

The postal inspector application process began in 1993, during my last semester in college, when I only had one month remaining before earning my bachelor's degree. The entire process took three whole years. As I recount these events of my life, I am amazed that I could put on such a game face and concentrate on my endeavors while being married to Dan. Dan, however, expected me to endure my relationship with him no matter his treatment of me. Why not? I allowed his behavior while we dated, including the apologizing, begging, and the making-up. Not one thing changed in our relationship after marriage. As a matter of fact, his behavior encouraged me to be just that much more driven to succeed!

Part IV – The Third Quarter

CHAPTER 11

Postal Inspector Academy

I began the third quarter of my career at the United States Postal Inspection Service law enforcement academy, where I would spend four months as a student postal inspector. *Again*, I faced possible heartbreak and disappointment if I failed a test or any portion of my training to keep my job. It was déjà vu!

This time I knew I would prevail through determination and preparation. My three-year journey to the academy began with extensive research. I was up for a challenge that was both mentally and physically demanding. I purchased and studied law enforcement manuals, took a gun safety course, and visited the local gun range for practice. I increased my strength and agility by working out with a physical trainer, lifting weights at least three to four times a week. As my endurance increased, I began incorporating 3-mile runs and was ecstatic about the 35-pound weight loss my commitment had rewarded me! I was ready to embark upon another, although markedly different, aspect of my career.

The first few weeks at the academy taught me the intricacies of the Postal Service audit and investigation processes. In late September 1996, after one month of training, we were surprised to learn that the US Postal Service Office of Inspector General (Postal IG) was created by Public Law 104-208 and passed by Congress. The timing of the announcement was terrible for both the students and the instructors at the academy. There was looming uncertainty among us as we wondered how the creation of the Postal IG would affect the future of the US Postal Inspection Service. Notwithstanding our confusion, training proceeded.

Initially, the Postal IG's purpose was to promote efficiency and cost effectiveness within the Postal Service. Comparatively, the Postal Inspection Service's role was to investigate internal crimes and external crimes. Internal crimes investigations focused on employees committing mail theft, embezzlement, and workers' compensation fraud. External crimes investigations focused on people external to the Postal Service, committing mail theft, utilizing the mail to transport drugs and other prohibited items through the mail, and business customers committing revenue fraud. Eventually, the Postal IG would increase their investigative role and responsibility and become another law enforcement agency for the Postal Service. The effects of the Postal IG would not be realized for another ten years.

Meanwhile, I visited my family once every four weeks. When home, I would check on the household expenses. It appeared that the bills were being paid timely. However, I noticed that the pre-dated checks, which I prepared in advance to pay the monthly bills while I was away, were deposited before the actual date written on the checks. I simply warned Dan that I did not have money to play catch up with the bills. The evidence of his cashing the checks early indicated that the money was probably being used for something else. But since the utilities were still on when I arrived home, I had no evidence to support my suspicions.

Dan was also never at the house when I called home to check on my daughter. He had promised to use the time that I was away to bond with my daughter. But that never happened. Upon speaking with my daughter, I simply asked her to make sure the doors were locked. I never doubted that my daughter was responsible and mature. My mother believed that Dan purposely stayed out late, hoping to force me to leave the academy. My mother assured me that she and my father would make sure my daughter had what she needed so that I could remain focused.

The four months in the academy was a great learning experience. The impromptu mental and physical challenges caused me little to no stress, as I was in excellent physical condition. So much so, that I engaged in the innate competition sparked in the areas of physical fitness, firearms, and test scores. Two male students led our runs. I ranked third among the six female students in my class during the runs. One time, I was so close to passing the female in second place that I could have touched her. If only, just that once, I had wiped that smug look off her face!

In preparation for our new jobs, we carried red handle firearms daily to familiarize those without prior law enforcement experience with wearing a gun and holster. During tactical firearms training, we carried weapons filled with blanks. I experienced a sympathetic reflex, which means one hand duplicates the actions of the other hand. While holding my weapon in my right hand and simultaneously using my left hand, I moved my left forefinger which caused my right forefinger to mock that action. Not realizing that my right forefinger was on the trigger, I accidentally discharged (shot) the weapon. Although I became an excellent marksman, the class never let me forget that accidental discharge (AD)! That incident would haunt me long after my graduation.

Defensive tactics (DT) were an integral part of our academy training. Sometimes the men in the class reverted to street moves instead of the textbook techniques we learned. Once, during one of our DT drills, the instructor thought he had gotten the best of me. He pinned me to the floor, and I pretended to accept defeat by allowing my body to become limp beneath him. Suddenly, I flipped him over and ended up on top! The class burst into uncontrollable laughter as they looked on because the instructor and the class had underestimated me. We often underestimated or overestimated one another during training.

There were eighteen student postal inspectors in my class. As I mentioned before, there were only six females. We lost one female trainee due to her non-performance. She lacked motivation and always had an excuse for not participating in group runs.

Speculation led us to believe the instructors voted her out! There were only four African American trainees, and I was one of the two females. After the Postal IG was appointed, we lost one African American male. Because our experiences were so demanding at times, it felt natural for the remaining three African American trainees to be drawn together by the common goal to succeed. We ran together on the weekends and studied together sometimes. It appeared that our friendships would extend beyond the academy. Not all of them did.

My father suddenly died of a heart attack during my last month of training. I immediately left the academy for one week. When I returned, I was no longer feeling any of it! I had not recovered from the shock of my father's death, and I was also distracted by other things going on at home. Although I had prayed to the Lord for help on my final exam, I did not pass it. In retrospect, I believe my prayers should have been more specific. Fortunately, we were allowed one make-up exam. Therefore, while everyone else was partying, I was confined to my room to study. While in my room, I remembered my mother telling me how proud my father was that I had made it to the academy. I was also struggling with the idea that my three years of preparation would have been for naught if I failed. Before I took the make-up exam, I prayed again, asking the Lord for total recall of information. When I passed, I said, *thank you, Lord!*

Post-graduation, we were all assigned to different offices throughout the United States. No two postal inspectors from our class worked in the same office. Fear of the unknown set in again. *Now what?* I doubted I had been told or taught enough about what to expect. The Postal IG was not mentioned again by our instructors after that first month of training. No one knew what was coming because of gaining an Inspector General. The competition among the former students evolved into competition among teams and teammates at our offices and continued throughout the remainder of my law enforcement career. Fortunately, *I* did not have another AD, real or pretend. Former friendships faded with the intrusion of politics and work-life situations — one particular friendship dissolved completely. Interestingly, my doubts were brought to the forefront as my probationary period began and ended, and my impending future revealed itself to me!

CHAPTER 12

The Early Days

I reported for duty in January 1997. One of my first conversations with my team leader (supervisor) was to answer, "Why did you become a postal inspector?" and "How did you prepare?" I replied that I became interested after seeing a recruitment poster. I prepared by researching and learning what I needed to accomplish becoming a postal inspector. He appeared to be impressed by my response. He told me that if I prepared in that manner throughout my career, I would continue to be successful. It was a very encouraging statement. But it was not entirely true. Perhaps in a perfect, unbiased, and non-political work environment it could have been true most of the time. But I could not help but wonder if he asked every new inspector those questions or was it just me. My team leader and most of my teammates were former Postal Service employees. So why was it so hard to believe that *I* did it?

Initially, I endured on-the-job training which encompassed spending several days on different teams observing real-time investigations and assisting when requested. Besides the fact that I was given assignments that no one else wanted, my training at the academy was more than adequate for the assistance I provided to the teams. My first crime lab submission was for a fingerprint analysis. I sorted through three garbage bags filled with rifled mail. I determined which torn pieces were most probable for latent fingerprints by imagining where the most pressure would be exerted to tear the envelopes. As a result, three suspects were identified. The first search warrant I supported was for a medical fraud case. I worked tirelessly searching for and seizing voluminous documents. I was verbally recognized for my thoroughness by the lead inspectors for both cases.

My first team assignment as an inspector was to investigate revenue fraud. After a couple of months, it was obvious that inspectors with a Postal Service background and *without* prior law enforcement experience were viewed somewhat differently than inspectors *with* prior law enforcement experience. Prior experience appeared to dictate team assignments. Although we received the same training, the stigma was there. Inspectors without prior law enforcement experience had to prove themselves by showing they could investigate external crimes.

Poetic Justice

In less than a year, I was moved to the audit team. The audit team was comprised of female inspectors who focused primarily on internal audit. Mary, our team leader was newly promoted. She was tough as nails and full of wit! She later became my mentor. Of course, the male inspectors did not want a female team leader or to perform audits. It paid the same, so why did it matter? It mattered because of the notoriety that criminal cases gained, not only in the press but also among peers within and outside the agency.

The audit team traveled a great deal, visiting postal facilities, and auditing postal processes and procedures. One day in 1997, while on assignment at headquarters, I was walking in the adjacent mall after lunch. Who did I see? Larry! Remember Larry? He was the manager who gave me my first detail opportunity, then *blocked* me from accepting my second. I followed Larry to his office, thinking how far up the career ladder he must have climbed to be housed at Postal Service headquarters. Well, I had made some progress too! I wanted to ensure Larry knew I too had arrived, despite his attempts to block me!

When I entered the office, I was greeted by Larry's secretary. I introduced myself and explained that I worked with Larry approximately 12 years prior. After the secretary spoke with Larry, she showed me to an interior office. I entered with a big smile.

Larry said, "And where do I know your smiling face from?"

I responded, "I'm the one who replaced the Express Mail coordinator in Florida while she was on maternity leave."

Larry's facial expression changed as he obviously remembered who I was and, I imagined, what had occurred between us. He was still so easy to read! I knew he remembered exactly what he had done and realized that he was not successful, *since* I was standing right in front of him. The fact that becoming an inspector was not just *any* position made my encounter with Larry that much sweeter! As I continued explaining that I was an inspector, Larry made small talk, naming a few inspectors, asking if I knew them. As I departed his office, I thought, *poetic justice!* I never saw Larry again. But that confrontation was such a liberating experience and confirmed the Lord answered another one of my unspoken prayers!

CHAPTER 13

Lautenberg Amendment

By 1997, Dan and I had been married for about four years and my daughter was almost 16 years old. Dan still had not taken any initiative to develop a relationship with her. He had come into our lives when she was six years old. I should have realized that if Dan had not done anything early on, he never would. I always blamed myself for overlooking how important it was for Dan to bond with my daughter *before* I married him.

One day at our house, it was discovered that an outside light by the French doors was broken. Dan accused my daughter of breaking it. I could not understand how he arrived at that conclusion. I immediately thought that the pool guy must have broken it when he was cleaning the pool and did not report it. But for some reason Dan insisted that my daughter had broken the light.

An argument began and I asked Dan to lower his voice because I knew that my daughter could hear. He said that he did not care. I became so angry that I left the house to cool down. But before I departed, Dan said, "I bet you wanted to hit me, but you thought about that paper those people had you sign."

I was astonished. A week or so prior to this argument, I disclosed to Dan that my management required me to sign a document regarding the Lautenberg Amendment. The Domestic Violence Offender Gun Ban – the Lautenberg Amendment, was enacted by the US Congress in 1996.

> *"It bans shipment, transport, ownership, and use of guns or ammunition by individuals convicted of misdemeanor domestic violence..."* (Wikipedia, 2017).

The Lautenberg Amendment exists across multiple public service occupations, including the medical and teaching professions. Therefore, my signature on the document indicated that I had no domestic charges or incidents. I was also agreeing that if I did, I would report it to management immediately. Potentially, I could have lost my job if I had any charges or incidents.

Dan's comment was jarring because I had not been thinking about hitting him. More importantly, I was concerned why my signing the document was on his mind. Was Dan, being fully aware of the consequences if a domestic violence incident occurred, trying to goad me into a physical altercation? Was that why the senseless argument began? Was Dan attempting to lure me into a situation where I would act in anger and hit him, and then suffer the consequences of losing my livelihood, after *he* reported *me* to the authorities?

Prayer:
Lord God, help us when we argue and fight within our families. Father, give us the discernment to recognize the ulterior motives and other underlying issues so that they can be addressed and controlled appropriately – before they become too big. Lord, help us to assess the damage and properly assist our children and other loved ones who are affected when physical and emotional altercations occur within the family. Father, we thank You, and we praise Your holy name, in Jesus' name we pray, amen.

Second Thoughts

During the last six months of 1997, I heard the Voice again. By this time, I knew the Voice belonged to the Spirit of the Lord. It happened during the final months of my five-year marriage. For several years, I watched my marriage fall apart. It was readily apparent that Dan had not embraced my becoming a law enforcement officer. He actually commented during one of our many arguments, "I didn't marry a postal inspector!"

When I spoke with other male friends, they were always complimentary and often stated how they would be proud of me if I were their spouse. Frankly, I never understood the implication that I was not supposed to progress in my career, and especially not in a law enforcement position.

Communicating with Dan had become more difficult, even more so when he became angry. His verbal abuse was often used as a defense mechanism. Somehow, we agreed to seek counseling to reconcile the marriage. However, once the counseling began, Dan was not receptive. He appeared to want the counselor to think I was the irrational one and would talk over me. After the second session, I was forced to accept that counseling was not going to help us. We *both* needed to be willing to accept the responsibility for our actions. I knew that another reconciliation with Dan, added to all the other reconciliations that had occurred in our relationship, was a waste of time.

Even though I was ready to dissolve the marriage, I still doubted my decision. As I continuously reviewed alternatives in my head, I heard the Spirit of the Lord say, "Didn't you do that already?"

I responded, "Yeah, but maybe I can ..."

"You did that too," the Spirit said.

I answered, "Okay."

I was finally able to put the Voice in perspective after this emotional decision to dissolve my marriage. I recognized that the Spirit counseled me during the most significant and emotionally charged moments in my life.

[47] He that is of God heareth God's words: ye therefore hear them not, because ye are not of God. (John 8:47 KJV)

It was in October 1997, while on one of many travel assignments for work, that Dan phoned me at the hotel and expressed his not wanting a divorce. I began to reconsider divorce. I thought that perhaps I had misjudged Dan and maybe he had matured, and I should give him another chance. Can you imagine that after all I had endured, I was rethinking divorce?

I was still deliberating by the time New Year's Eve 1997 had arrived. A friend of mine extended a last-minute invitation to a gathering. Attempting to do the right thing, I phoned Dan's job to advise him that we (my daughter and I) would not be at home when he arrived from work. To my surprise, the supervisor informed me that Dan was not at work and had been scheduled off for the entire day.

I was livid! I could not even enjoy myself at the party. When we finally returned home, Dan was awaiting us, pretending that he had just arrived from work. He had the nerve to have an attitude because we were not at home! Dan began questioning me as to my whereabouts. I responded, "If you had been at work, you would have known where we were!" In response to his deceit, I said, "I had considered not divorcing you, but there is not a 'expletive' thing you can do to make me stay with you!"

During the next two months, I began packing Dan's things because he was not taking the initiative to do it himself. He acted as if I was going to change my mind. I went to Office Depot and purchased a divorce packet filled with several documents. I completed the entire packet and laid it on the kitchen counter for him to review. I also purchased a quit claim deed for Dan to execute because he had agreed to accept several thousand dollars in exchange for the transfer of his interest in our home to me. When we went before the notary, I purposely ensured that we signed the divorce papers first, and then conducted the financial transaction and completed the quit claim deed. I had a feeling in my gut that if we had completed the quit claim deed first, Dan would have refused to sign the divorce papers, taken my money, and run!

Prayer:

Heavenly Father, thank You for the Comforter, who answers when we call and guides us through the storms of life. We want to grow closer to You and open the lines of communication so that we can hear when You speak to us. Lord, we want to discover that place where we can sense Your presence, hear You and receive the peace and calm that only You bring to our spirit. Father, we thank You for being that steady Rock needed for real-time support and courage. Lord, we are forever grateful, and we praise Your holy name, in Jesus' name we pray, amen.

The Purge

In March 1998, during the 45 days before Dan and I divorced, I invited him to a restaurant for dinner. We discussed our upcoming divorce proceedings at the courthouse. I knew it would be our last encounter, our last date. When I drove home from the restaurant tears began to flow from my eyes. I was in disbelief because although I was crying, I was not upset. I was perplexed by the demonstration of sorrow because I was actually elated and somewhat relieved that I was finally divorcing Dan.

When I arrived at home, I called my mother and told her that tears had poured from my eyes although I had not felt any sorrow. She said that I had been with Dan for a long time, and it was perfectly normal to expect that I would be upset at this juncture. I insisted that I was not upset and told her that my crying simply did not make sense to me. That was the first time in my life that after presenting my mother with an issue, problem, or concern I was experiencing, she did not have an answer or a solution for me.

I remained perplexed until sometime later, when I again spoke with my good friend, Pat, and described to her what had happened to me. Pat had become an evangelist and would often offer spiritual guidance to me. She told me that it was *my spirit* that had cried. If this sounds peculiar to you, imagine how strange it was for me! I had experienced a separate part of me crying. I had to agree with Pat. I realized that my spirit had mourned the demise of my marriage.

Dissolution of Marriage

In exactly 45 days, Dan and I were scheduled for a hearing with the judge to finalize the divorce. I invited a friend to accompany me as my witness. When Dan did not show up, I thought to myself, *this is a piece of cake!* But the judge instructed me to call Dan and required me to wait for him. When Dan finally arrived, he appeared aggravated.

While in the judge's chamber, Dan was uncooperative and his tone, embarrassing. The judge asked me if I was requesting any support from him. I responded that because Dan and I had no children together, I was not.

"What did she say!?" he yelled. It seemed that because he was sitting in the back of the judge's chamber, he did not hear the question.

I repeated the judge's question, "She asked if I was requesting any support from you, and I said no."

Dan said, "What? Support? You should be giving me support. You make more money than I do!"

Oh, my Lord! He's attempting to sabotage the divorce proceedings.

The judge appeared to change her demeanor and asked, "Have you been intimate?"

I responded, "No ma'am."

I remembered reading in the divorce packet about consummation and was reminded about Dan calling me almost every day during the 45 days, asking me to sleep with him. I consistently said, *no*, because I had no intention of allowing any physical relationship to ensue after filing for divorce. I had not even thought that it could be perceived as reconciliation until that precise moment.

I do not exactly recall what the judge asked, but Dan responded, "I may have signed them (divorce papers), but I didn't know what I was signing."

My head spun around very quickly to look at Dan, realizing that he was accusing me of coercing him to sign the divorce papers. I began to pray. I asked God that if He allowed me to get out of the marriage, I would never hastily marry again.

The judge then turned her attention to me, and I said, "Your honor, I just gave him $10,000 in return for his signing a quit claim deed. He has already used the money to put a down payment on another house!"

The judge was unmoved. She looked as if she was thinking, *so what!* So, I prayed some more.

Finally, after some moments of what seemed like eternal silence, the judge said to Dan, "If you didn't know what you were signing, why did you sign the Answer?"

Again, Dan responded, "I may have signed it, but I didn't know what I was signing."

I had no idea what the "Answer" was. There was more silence, but this time the judge said, "Well, if you had not signed the Answer, I would not have granted this divorce. But because you signed the Answer, I will grant this divorce."

I heard the gavel hit the desk and I said under my breath, *thank you, Jesus!*

As we departed the courthouse, my friend stated, "I thought that lady was not going to give you your divorce."

I said, "Me too!"

I was sure that the judge seriously contemplated denying the divorce. I knew the Lord heard me and answered my prayers.

The divorce packet included the Answer, and when I reviewed the packet again, I saw that we signed it. I learned later that the Answer is sometimes delivered or presented separate from the actual divorce paperwork. Our signatures indicated that we agreed, and it prevailed.

Prayer:
Father, thank You for the instant replay when we are making important decisions. Lord, many times we second guess ourselves, believing that our decisions may not be the right or best ones. Father, only You give us that epiphany – allowing us to see what we need to, when we need to. Father, we love You and praise Your holy name, in Jesus' name we pray, amen.

Instant Replay

Dan

It seemed like I had Stockholm syndrome, which is not too far from the truth. Dan became intertwined with my soul. When this happens with a mate, it is extremely difficult to make the best decisions. But, when the Spirit of the Lord intervenes and convinces you that you have done all you can, and enough is enough, you will find the strength and determination to make firm decisions.

When the 45 days of separation began, Dan constantly phoned me asking to spend the night with me and I consistently said, *no*! In response to my saying '*no*' to one of his last requests to sleep with me, Dan responded, "I guess I am out of your system." I have always remembered his statement. It confirmed for me that many men know that they become a part of a woman's system. I was ready to start anew because I had done all I could for my marriage. But when I departed that restaurant, knowing I would not intentionally see Dan again, my spirit purged him from my system all on its own.

Dan did not know how to show love outside of having sex. Dan believed that he did not need to change and that I would never leave him. That day in the judge's chamber, God reminded me of the conniving person Dan really was. The bet was the first sign! No matter the circumstances, Dan and I had made an agreement. He had every opportunity to reconcile our marriage before we arrived at that juncture. Instead, Dan continued to deceive me. Even when he took my money in return for the quit claim deed, he still attempted to manipulate the situation.

At some point, I recognized the consistent phone calls to convince me to spend the night with him and the outbursts in the judge's chamber were the result of his being coached. It was indeed a conspiracy! If I had allowed Dan to sleep with me, I would have had to admit to the judge that we consummated the marriage after I filed for divorce. The judge would have surely denied the divorce.

During our relationship, I told Dan about my mother's 'don't eat your vomit' advice once or twice. He would often taunt me, "*you gon' be eating your vomit!*" I would answer him every time, "*oh no I won't be!*" Sadly, I had already eaten my vomit too many times during my relationship with Dan. But when enough was enough, I was finally able to leave the *vomit* on the floor!

CHAPTER 14

The Façade

Two months after my divorce, I was at a local NOBLE (National Organization of Black Law Enforcement Officers) dinner and dance with several co-workers. Once the formal dinner was over and the dancing began, a police officer named Troy approached me. Troy had a dark complexion and was at least 6'5" tall. His eyes were brown and round, and his lips, full. He had very little hair on his face, but the hair on his head was cut in a high-top fade. Troy was impeccably groomed and dressed very nicely. He must have made a good impression on me because we exchanged numbers that night. Apparently, one of my female co-workers thought he was attractive too because I received much attitude from her about the attention Troy gave me!

After our initial contact, Troy and I spent several hours getting acquainted over the phone. I recalled hearing what I thought was a garage door opening and closing. That sound led me to believe that Troy had a place of his own. That quality was of major importance to me after my previous courtship and marriage. I had a good feeling about him because he appeared to have it all together.

On one of our first dates, Troy wore nice clothes, shoes, and accessories. However, the accessories were a little extravagant and often unnecessary. For example, when we went to a comedy show, he wore fashion eyewear. Another time, Troy showed me a leather briefcase that he sometimes carried. I wondered why a cop who wore a uniform needed a leather briefcase.

Our second or third date was at one of his friends' home. His friend was married, and he and his wife had a very nice home. This one night, we watched a video entitled, "No More Sheets," by Juanita Bynum, a televangelist. In this video, Bynum described that a purging should occur when a relationship dissolves or dies. Bynum noted that prayer could accomplish this purging. She suggested that women really cannot move on to the next relationship because remnants of the last relationship would prevent them from moving forward, further explaining that the desire for the man would still be within her spirit. Bynum commented that men lost (some) strength when their relationships dissolved.

After watching this video, I had an epiphany! I could not believe that I was receiving confirmation regarding what had happened to me after parting from Dan at the restaurant. It was surreal. Troy later told me that his friend had observed my reaction to the video and recognized that I "connected" with it. I thought it necessary to give Troy an explanation. So, I told him what I experienced just a couple of months prior, right before divorcing Dan. Troy said, "Thank you, for sharing with me that you purged."

Troy's reaction to my personal experience with purging stuck with me because he appeared to think it a green light to pursue a commitment with me. After only one more date, Troy began pressuring me to commit by saying, "Let's do a blueprint!" As I considered his proposition, it dawned on me that Troy had not even invited me to his home! I wanted him to *voluntarily* invite me to visit him, not coerce him. Realistically, I was apprehensive about a commitment so soon after my divorce.

I continued to spend time with Troy because he was nice to me, and I hoped that we could be compatible. Troy was also polite to my daughter. As illustration, he allowed her to interview him for a school assignment. Just knowing that my daughter was comfortable enough to ask Troy for help gave me some comfort. I hoped he could be good for us both.

I had begun to look forward to spending time with Troy. But he often used our moments alone to express being uncomfortable since we had not yet been intimate. It was very annoying. Once, I was sitting on his lap and he said, "You know I am a man..." Was that really necessary? Why couldn't he enjoy the moment?

When we finally discussed having sex, I told Troy I thought our first time would be like "fireworks," believing it would represent a culmination of emotions. I just wanted it to be special. I did not expect another man to be like Dan in bed, but I hoped to feel excited about the moment – before and after.

The night of intimacy finally arrived, and it was planned – which was a huge mistake! Troy took me to this hotel that was for adults only. The rooms were decorated with mirrors on the ceiling and the walls were red! The room also had a heart-shaped bed covered with a red bedspread. The lighting was also purposely dimmed. It was not what I would have wanted or expected for my first time with him. I was not impressed. I guess it was Troy's fantasy because it certainly was not mine!

I believe Troy tried hard to impress me. When he removed his clothing, he posed for me as if showing off his nude physique. The entire scene ruined my mood. I was not excited, nor could I fake it. My disposition probably made Troy nervous because he behaved as if he did not know what to do. I think he was accustomed to women being more aggressive with him.

To make matters worse, the sex was disappointing. I could not help but sense he was expecting me to participate in oral sex with him, something he had once referred to as "scans." As I observed his awkward movements and felt his uncertain touch, I said to Troy, "I am just like any other woman." But maybe I was not. Although he experienced an orgasm, I did not. He even dropped the used condom on the floor. Who does that?

Despite the awful sexual encounter with Troy, I tried to chalk it up to first-time jitters. The next time we were together, Troy asked if "it" (referring to sex) was going to happen again. I responded, "I don't know."

I truly did not know. I was still stuck on his constantly coming to my house, instead of his inviting me to his.

Troy finally invited me to where he lived but only because I insisted. I was perplexed as we approached a gated apartment community. I remembered the garage door opening sound, so I expected to see a single-family home or townhome. While walking toward the front door, I experienced some anxiety. Once he opened the door, I knew why. The apartment was barely furnished and appeared to have one bedroom. The living room area only had one couch and the television sat on a box! While standing in the foyer, I could see the clothing that he had worn on our most recent date hanging on the bedroom door in a clear plastic dry-cleaning bag.

I took only a couple of steps to view the kitchen, which was close to the entrance. The kitchen showed very little signs of use and the countertops were bare. I was so alarmed at the appearance of the apartment that I did not walk any further than the front door and kitchen area. After my observations, I became suspicious as to whether the apartment was truly his. I was extremely uncomfortable, and I said, "Take me home."

When we arrived at my home, we stood on the front porch and Troy again asked me about a commitment. I did not feel that it was an easy decision, and I thought it should have been. I could not ignore remembering the sound of a garage door opening or closing during that earlier conversation with him. *Where was he then? Was 'his apartment' one of those group leased places I had previously heard about? The ones where married and attached police officers took women? Did that garage door belong to a home that he shared with a wife or significant other? Or was I just the next woman that he wanted to move in with?* So, as we stood there, he looked at me and waited for an answer. I told him, "I'll think about it."

Either that night or the following night, I dreamed I was at my old job, working as a supervisor for the post office. That position required me to dress professionally, however in the dream I could see that my clothes were raggedy. I awakened knowing the dream had revealed the truth behind Troy's façade. I phoned my mother and told her about the dream. She said that I should ask the Spirit of the Lord to show me the dream again and reveal its meaning. I did and had the exact same dream again! I was convinced after having the dream the second time that Troy was not who he seemed. Most compelling was that my clothes were in stark contrast to what Troy's clothes were in the natural. *God will clarify things for you if you ask!*

I phoned Troy and asked him to meet me at the neighborhood mall. I was not sure how to explain to Troy that my dream was deciding our fate. So, I decided to tell him the truth, that the dream made me feel uncomfortable about my continuing to date him. Troy was caught by surprise and desperately wanted to hear about the dream, he said "Tell *me* the dream."

I was certain he would not comprehend its meaning as I did. For this reason, I decided not to share the dream with him. Even though I told Troy that we could go out sometime if he wanted, I knew I would not change my mind about the role he would play in my life. I guess Troy knew it too because he never called me again.

I had two chance encounters with Troy in the years that followed. The first was approximately five years later in a Walgreens drug store parking lot. It was early in the morning before daybreak. While in the store, I noticed an unfamiliar and strikingly tall man standing in line, towering over those around him. Once outside the store, a police car nearly hit me as I crossed into the parking lot. I got into my car and began to drive but noticed that the police car had not moved. I decided to approach the car, and when I did, I recognized the driver as Troy. Only then did he motion me to stop and started a conversation by complimenting the old model Mercedes I was driving.

The second encounter was about a year later during a rather large event held at an auditorium. I was sitting in the center balcony area, and I could see Troy in the lower level still towering over the crowd around him. I assumed he was performing an off-duty assignment. It was unbelievable that while descending the steps and exiting the auditorium, I caught a glimpse of Troy in my peripheral vision to my right. It seemed that all the people were gone, and it was just him and me. Troy turned his back in my direction and pretended not to see me, so I ignored him.

Prayer:

Heavenly Father, thank You for Your divine intervention into our lives. Many times, things happen, and we are perplexed. Father, we want to open lines of communication with You and ask for clarification about the situations in our lives. Lord, we want to recognize the way You speak to us, whether it is through our dreams or by other means. Father, we are working on being receptive to You and we humbly ask that You make it plain. Father, too often we are in a hurry and must learn that we need to achieve a better understanding before we make decisions. Lord, we want to believe the first person, place or thing that comes our way is good. Therefore, we ask for discernment because what looks good on the outside is many times not good. Father, we love You and we praise You, in Jesus' name, amen.

Again?

Remember Freddie? Of course, you do! Freddie was the man with the revolving door, the one whose house at which I was caught by one of his girlfriends! Approximately ten years after our affair, Freddie and I were communicating via email. Around that time, AOL (America Online) was the new email communication. Freddie was always witty, making idle chit-chat. It was only once or twice he showed his feelings. In one of his emails, he asked me, "You ready to get married?"

I thought, *that again?* But I quickly responded, "You aren't the marrying kind!"

Then, in another email he wrote, "You used me!"

I am sure the comment referred to our past secret rendezvous. I thought, *What?! Who was using who?*

Sometime later, I traveled quite a bit in the late 90s, and I met Freddie for dinner once while working in the city where he lived. I recall that at dinner, Freddie made a comment that began with, "When we dated..."

I interjected, "We never dated!"

He responded, "Oh, we just saw each other."

I said, "Yep!"

After dinner, when he dropped me at my hotel and walked me to my room, he seemed to wait expectantly, but he was waiting for an invitation that would not come. Too much time had passed for anything other than just dinner and conversation. I did not bother to explain that it was not going to be that kind of evening. But Freddie got the message and departed after a few minutes.

When Freddie finally came to my town, and I am sure he visited often since his mother was still local, he finally called me. We planned what I thought was a real date. I was actually a little nervous and somewhat excited. It had been over 10 years since our affair. It would have really been something different for us to have an actual date.

I waited for Freddie to either arrive or call me with the specifics. But he never showed up or called. When it became obvious to my then 17-year-old daughter that I had been stood up, she approached me where I was sitting and said, "Ma, I don't like him!"

As I sat there, tears began to fall uncontrollably from my eyes. Again, I was not upset, but I was definitely crying. I then asked myself, *him too?* I could not believe I was purging again! I had not realized until that day that Freddie was still a part of my spirit – even after all those years!

Prayer:
Heavenly Father, help us with purging so that we will no longer be held captive in a bad relationship or by memories or remnants of those that have ended. Lord, help us to understand, and to help others understand that sometimes spiritual things happen that we cannot explain or even understand. Father, we are learning that if we seek answers and sometimes even when we don't, You graciously grant us the understanding that we need, at the time that we need it – if it is Your will. Lord, we thank You and we praise Your holy name, in Jesus' name we pray, amen.

Instant Replay

The Façade

My relationship with Troy had barely even started, but he had time to prepare his home for my visit, *if* he really thought of me as someone special and knew he needed a home of his own. The alternative should have been to be honest with me about not having a place of his own, or at least explaining what was going on in his life before we met.

However, Troy using his friend's home for our dates was a blessing in disguise. There is no doubt in my mind that seeing the Bynum video was more than just a coincidence. It confirmed that my purging experience was all that I understood it to be – a release from Dan. Although I agreed wholeheartedly with Bynum about asking the Lord for release to assist with purging, my spirit mourned/purged the demise of my marriage with Dan all on its own.

Perhaps running into Troy twice those five or so years later were opportunities to reconcile. Yet Troy behaved so ridiculously both times when he refused to initiate a conversation with me. I am sure he wanted me to speak to him first because I had rejected him so long ago. Although I entertained his conversation during the first encounter, once he turned his back to me on the second encounter, I felt no need to speak with him.

Again?

My involvement with Freddie those years prior surely kept me from meeting someone more worthy of my time. It did not help that my experiences with commitment and marriage had been unpleasant. Granted, initially I did not want a commitment with Freddie. But seeing him again, after my second divorce, my needs and desires had changed. Therefore, I wanted more from Freddie and any other man that approached me under the guise of pursuing a relationship with me, sexual or otherwise.

A little over 30 years after our affair, Freddie contacted me and said he was separated. Once he gave me some details about the issues in his marriage, I told him they could work it out. Another two years passed, and Freddie said he was newly divorced. I imagined he wanted to rekindle something we never really had. He even gave me an impressive, verbal financial resume!

A month or so later, his knowing I was a licensed realtor, we communicated regarding his interest in some real estate. In follow-up, I texted him, but the conversation took a sharp turn when he asked if I was seeing someone. That question was expected. But when I responded, "No," I did not expect him to say,

"I think we should [get together] for old time-sake."

"Of course, you do. But I don't!" I responded.

What was even more disappointing was that he told me that the older a woman became, the harder it was for her to find a man, adding that men do not want women with "too many miles," referring to a woman's age. I saw it as a manipulation tactic to convince me that as a woman aged, her opportunities to find a man would diminish. He insinuated older women should settle for less than what they wanted because of their age. I tried to turn the text conversation around, but eventually, I received another text,

"I think we should [have sex]."

I quickly responded, "No, thank you, we will not repeat the same type of relationship." *I will not be eating my vomit!*

"He texted, "Think about it."

I texted, "Nope!"

He texted, "Okay."

... And the Fat Lady sang!

CHAPTER 15

Selective Integrity

I met Todd in 1998, while working on a joint investigation with another agent at his office. As I departed through the lobby, I noticed him staring at me. The agent introduced us, and I learned Todd was also a law enforcement officer. He later told me that from the moment he saw me, he thought, "I can be with her!"

We exchanged business cards and began to talk quite often. I invited him to a couple of office functions, and he was well liked by my colleagues. We went to the movies a couple of times. I still remember that our first movie date was to see *Love and Basketball*, which is still one of my favorites. We also frequented restaurants and went to the beach. I felt us becoming closer. Over the next two years, we built a friendship that I believed would grow into something more.

I anxiously waited for Todd to initiate a serious relationship with me. I would scream to myself, s*ay something!* while with him. It seemed strange that we were moving at such a slow pace. Todd finally invited me to an office event. It was an annual football tournament between his agency's Florida offices. His office was winning, and he wanted me to attend. They were in Cocoa Beach, FL, which meant I would have to drive five hours north. I was excited because I believed it signified the transition of our relationship to more than just friends. I decided to leave on the following day.

The next morning, I awoke and got dressed for the game. I checked on my teenaged daughter (who was usually still sleeping at that hour), and she was not there! *She must have departed before the crack of dawn.* My first reaction was panic, but upon further thought I realized that she purposely departed early. Afterall, she was in high school with her own car. I called her cell phone, and she did not answer. I spoke with my mother and sister, and they had not seen or heard from her either. I grew even angrier once I resolved that she snuck out of the house to be with her boyfriend. Instead of sitting at home, going out of my mind, and waiting for her to call, I decided to go to Cocoa Beach. I spent the entire five-hour drive and the remainder of the day periodically calling her cell phone. In retrospect, I should have stayed home.

I arrived at the football game by half time. Todd's team lost. I followed Todd and his teammates back to the hotel. Once there, I watched Todd's roommate scramble around, gathering his things. I could only surmise that he had not planned to leave on that day and my arrival pushed him to leave earlier. Shortly thereafter, my daughter called. I gave her a few choice words and was finally able to truly relax. We went to dinner, picked up a movie, and returned to the hotel.

As we watched the movie, I laid my head on Todd's lap and he caressed my hair. The movie reminded Todd of an undercover operation he participated in, and he recounted the details of that operation as we watched the movie. It was obvious that he was proud of his contribution to the operation's success. Everything seemed so perfect!

There were two beds in the hotel room, and I still wish I had chosen to sleep alone. However, I thought that we would finally have a serious relationship. Afterall, Todd had invited me to spend time with him amongst his friends and co-workers. It had to mean something, right?

We began to kiss passionately. Then, Todd suddenly stopped kissing me, looked into my eyes, and said, "Wait, I have a girlfriend!"

Todd explained that although he loved me, he had been waiting for me to say something. Todd said he had just begun the relationship. All I heard was that he loved me. I assumed he would break things off with this other woman. Therefore, I allowed him to continue kissing me. I had never been kissed like that before. It was the best kiss I had ever experienced. However, between Todd's lackluster foreplay and blunders with the condom, I was extremely disappointed with the sexual experience. The absence of passion and intimacy made the act a total waste of my time. But since I cared for him, I hoped it would be better the next time.

During the trip home, I relished the thoughts of what I believed was a budding relationship. The following week, I learned that Todd had no intention of breaking up with his girlfriend. Although he had been open and honest with me about her, he had not been open and honest with her about me. I remember confiding in a friend about the situation and she advised that I "arm myself" if I wanted to be a willing participant in a "love triangle".

I asked Todd why he had invited me to the game instead of his girlfriend. He said they were winning, and he just wanted me there. I was puzzled by his logic. He admitted that he had purposely hidden his relationship from me. Todd said he knew I would not have gone out with him had I known he had a girlfriend.

"Where is your integrity?" I asked.

It was an obvious soft spot with him, being that he was this accomplished law enforcement officer. It hurt and offended him that I had questioned his integrity. It was apparent that his integrity was selective. I realized that I had put him on a pedestal. I could not believe that he was capable of such deceit.

I tried hopelessly to get Todd to rectify the situation, believing he would do right by me. He seemed to think there was nothing wrong with continuing our "friendship" despite his having a girlfriend. I waited for days, hoping that Todd would apologize to me and sever ties with his girlfriend. But it never happened.

Our communication was no longer the same. Todd would call, but the conversations were strained, I did not know what to say to him. This continued for several weeks until one day he called after midnight and told me that he could not sleep. I asked, "Where are you?"

He answered, "Around the corner from your house."

Although I was not sure what to expect, I allowed him to come over.

As we sat on my bedroom floor, I watched Todd struggle with his words. He had awakened me yet had no words of value. At some point, he told me that he had not known that his feelings for me had been reciprocated and admitted that he had been protecting himself from being hurt by me. As he held me, I became uncomfortable and disgusted when I realized he was aroused. It was the last time I allowed him to visit me.

After that night, I stopped answering Todd's phone calls. I cried for three sleepless nights. Even my little Shih Tzu sensed my pain and sat at my feet attempting to provide comfort. Todd had broken my heart. Until then, I had not realized that I was in love.

During the next five years, Todd would call my office asking to meet me for lunch. He would say, "I thought enough time had passed..."

I would respond, "No, enough time has not passed."

I maintained my distance and was able to heal. At one point, Todd called and said he had broken up with his girlfriend. By then, I was in a relationship. He asked me the difference between my boyfriend and him. I responded, "He knows his limitations and is honest about it."

One day, my daughter had an urgent matter which required a truck. Todd was the only person I knew with a truck and who would help on short notice. I called and he responded immediately. We finally had that meal. I told Todd that he had repaired our friendship because he was willing to help me.

Fifteen or so years passed, and Todd and I remained friends. He never stopped saying that he loved me. Which is probably why twice during the years, I still wondered if we could be together. But Todd seemed to always have a girlfriend. Unless I asked Todd a direct question regarding his relationship status, I would not have known. Once I accepted that he would not change, I no longer had any expectations for us. Eventually, I told Todd that I did not trust him with my heart, and we were better as friends.

Todd married his last girlfriend, another woman that I knew nothing about until approximately four years before they were married. When I learned about her, it was like reliving the deceit all over again, and it still hurt. I did not understand why he chose to continuously keep his relationships from me. However, Todd had given me the answer long ago – he believed our friendship would not have been the same.

Instant Replay

The Lord gave me an opportunity to stay home when my daughter was missing, but my stubbornness and anger pushed me to drive to Cocoa Beach anyway. Todd and I were intimate only once. The heart ache and pain I experienced forced me to recognize that he was indeed my *vomit*. The crying that occurred during the three days of insomnia was a *purging*, which prepared me for the five-year reprieve. Eventually, I felt no need to talk with him.

When we finally reconciled, I *managed* my vomit by controlling our interactions, making no assumptions, and asking direct questions. However, because our friendship seemed so great, I still pondered, *can he be the one, even after all of that?* Our friendship survived because I was forced to see that Todd would never change. As a result, I no longer had any false expectations.

My relationship with Todd allowed me to *thrive* as I met other men. He taught me that with some men, there is a big difference between the women they will love and the women they will marry. I had no doubt that Todd loved me. I was just not the wife for him – and that was fine with me!

CHAPTER 16

Dismayed

It was the year 2000. Another four years had passed, and I made one final effort to assist Danny in creating a relationship with his daughter. I spoke with Danny while she was preparing for college. I hoped he would finally make up for the lost years with my daughter by being supportive in some way and maybe provide her a computer and some mature communication.

To my dismay, he responded, "I'll help you with her if you date me." He added, "I'll rent this house (referring to his own home) and move in with you." By this time, he had divorced.

At this point, the conversation was one-sided because I was speechless from shock. Then I heard him say, "You took her and left me." As if my actions somehow exonerated him as a parent during the past years.

I became very angry and expressed some choice expletives regarding his suggestion. Then I said, "Unless it is about the well-being of my child, don't call me!" It was the last time I spoke with Danny.

The Three Sisters - Conclusion

In 2000, it had been two years since Dan and I had divorced. It was then that I learned what really happened the night Betty allegedly shot herself. One of my friends decided to break her silence. She had previously worked at the location of the shooting and was living in another state. Her sister, who was local and also worked for the post office, told her what happened.

One evening, during a conversation with my friend, she decided to enlighten me. She began by saying, "Since you are divorced now, I can tell you this."

She asked me if Dan had ever told me about a shooting incident. I told her, "Yes," and commenced to tell her Dan's version of the story.

My friend responded, "Child, that was his girlfriend. They were arguing and she pulled a gun on him." She added, "He was the biggest whore out there!"

She could sense that I was taken aback by that information and responded to my unspoken question. She explained that because she divorced her husband after being told he cheated on her, she did not want to be responsible for causing me to divorce. I told her that I would have divorced Dan sooner if she had told me. I had mixed feelings about her delay in telling me such pivotal information, but she was 10 years my senior. I believed she acted out of love.

During the two years following my divorce, Dan periodically asked me on dates. Instead of awaiting his next call, I initiated a conversation and said, "I bet you thought I would never find out what really happened to Jo's sister the night of the shooting. Now I know why you and Jo had become such good friends, her sister was your girlfriend!"

Dan's response was, "You always want to believe the worst about me."

Dan never admitted his affair; but he ceased asking me on dates.

[32] But a man who commits adultery has no sense; whoever does so destroys himself. (Proverbs 6:32 NIV)

Instant Replay

Dismayed

It is unfortunate, but some parents really feel that if they are not with the other parent, they are not obligated to do anything for their children. In retrospect, I believe Danny's behavior was about inadvertently hurting me, and our child was just collateral damage. It was easy for Danny to discern that a relationship between him and my child was important to me because he knew I had a relationship with my father, one that I valued greatly. My consistent efforts to assist their relationship were clearly motivated by how important my relationship with my own father was to me. I am sure this was obvious to Danny.

As parents, you want your children to have everything you had and more. I wanted my child and Danny to have a relationship that resembled the one I had with my father. Despite Danny's behavior, that could have created a void, my child later told me that because of the relationship she had with my father – her grandfather, she did not feel that she had missed anything in Danny's absence. She said my father had given her what she needed. My child had what I had after all!

The Three Sisters

I had finally gotten clarity regarding the things that puzzled me prior to and around the time of the shooting incident. Dan's newfound friendship with Jo had always nagged me; as did Sue's reaction to my inquiry about Betty's wellbeing.

However, regarding the shooting incident, I was given discernment, but ignored the implications that something was amiss. It was logical for anyone in that situation to be distressed, Betty could have been seriously hurt. I wish I had asked questions about Dan. I am sure someone would have eagerly supplied the answers, but I was too trusting.

Prayer:

Father, we thank You for discernment. Lord, we learn that even when we know that things are not what they seem, our destiny dictates the timing of all things. Father, we ask for enlightenment at the right time, so that we can address our situations in a timely and most appropriate manner. Lord, we know that we become stronger as we face life's disappointments and that sometimes You purposely keep things from us and reveal them in Your timing.

Father, we accept Your plans for our lives. Lord, we thank You and we praise Your holy name, in Jesus' name we pray, amen.

CHAPTER 17

Politics and 9-11

The first ramification of the creation of the Postal IG was when audit was eliminated from the Postal Inspection Service and re-established by the Postal IG. Consequently, I returned to investigating revenue fraud. One year I made three arrests – arrests were good! That was more arrests than anyone on my team and I was not recognized, as others had been before. My three arrests even got the attention of the first in command, the Inspector in Charge (INC). He called me to his office and asked how I had accomplished such a feat. I answered, "Partnering with local law enforcement." I had learned to work smarter, not harder! You see, my suspects were not only committing crimes against the Postal Service, but other crimes too!

Do you remember where you were on September 11, 2001? I was sitting at my desk when my team leader appeared at my office doorway and said, "They are attacking the World Trade Center." At that time, I had never visited New York City and as I stood up and headed for the conference room TV, my mind raced, *where is the World Trade Center?* As I watched that second plane collide into the second Twin Tower, I knew I had witnessed an intentional attack! While the events of that day were captured on national TV news, I was acutely aware that my "federal" law enforcement job did not compare to the jobs of the public servants who risked and lost their lives on that day helping others.

Many people had not even heard of a postal inspector until a week later, on or about September 18, 2001, when the anthrax attacks began. Being an inspector in Florida provided the opportunity to respond to anthrax suspicions and threats. However, the Inspection Service appeared to assert that inspectors were expendable (and maybe we were), dispatching us to any post office having sightings of white powder and disseminating the drug ciprofloxacin or "cipro" in case we breathed in anthrax germs. My first appearance on the local news was after I responded to an anthrax call at a Florida post office. News reporters were outside of the post office video recording while we were departing. I often wished I had requested a copy of the footage to show my grandchildren!

Training at the academy did not prepare me for the case that I developed which was never prosecuted. While in training, I believed that if I developed a case or solved a crime, I could simply arrest the suspect, present the case for prosecution, and justice would prevail. However, there were even politics involved with getting suspects arrested and cases prosecuted.

My first experience with the *who-you-know* politics of the legal system was when my first criminal case never got the attention it deserved. It was a revenue fraud case involving writing bad checks to the Postal Service to buy stamps. The stamps were then sold at half-price or less to local convenience stores. I quantified lost revenue of almost $50,000 and identified 42 suspects. The state prosecutor promised to issue arrest warrants for the six ring leaders, from which I identified the additional 36 suspects through familial and other relationships. I also interviewed two of the suspects who confirmed what my investigation had disclosed.

I presented the case to the state attorney, and she appeared to be eager to prosecute the case. I believed it was the case that would have showcased my investigative skills and strongly supported my future promotional endeavors. After I visited the state attorney at least three times, it was inconceivable that she was not interested in prosecuting my case. My team leader finally accompanied me to meet with her a fourth time, believing it would have encouraged her to issue the arrest warrants, but his intervention was also unsuccessful.

Fight Like a [Big] Girl!

Threat Management encompassed firearms training and defensive tactics. Firearm qualifications were performed semi-annually and required shooting 50 rounds (bullets) at the targets placed at the 3, 5, 7, 10, 15, and 25-yard lines, passing with a score of no less than 75%. I practiced with a bullseye at least once in between qualifications to maintain passing scores. Using a bullseye helped to hone my skills, evident whenever we performed creative drills during qualifications. Once, we fired at bowling pins from the 10 and 15-yard lines. When I was able to shoot them, in comparison to the other inspectors who could not, I realized how effective practicing with the bullseye was. Another time, we fired at balloons after we blew them up and stapled them to the targets. I recall that day being very windy, which made the balloons even more difficult to shoot. I was amazed that I shot the balloons even while they were bouncing around on the targets!

We had one female inspector who always made 100% at firearms qualifications, which was very impressive. I asked her how she did it. She said, "I learned right the first time." However, when that same inspector experienced an accidental discharge (AD), it was extremely embarrassing for her, and understandably so. An AD could possibly injure or even kill the one who has it or someone else. ADs had to be reported immediately to the INC. Talk of the AD occurrence spread like wildfire throughout the many Inspection Service offices. One of my academy classmates residing in a completely different state, rumored that it was *I* who had the AD, just because I had experienced an AD while at the academy. When I learned that people thought it was me, I shook my head in disbelief. I remembered one of the cardinal rules of firearms safety, simply stated – *keep your finger off the trigger until you are ready to shoot*. Now I learned *that* right the first time!

Defensive tactics training was annual. There was one defensive tactics drill we often practiced for one minute while our opponent wore red-man gear. Red-man gear was red and similar in thickness to those old gym mats that were in high school gyms years ago. It was configured to conform to certain areas of the body for protection from kicks and strikes. Our opponent was an inspector who wore the red-man gear. Once I fought the opponent using defensive kicks and baton strikes for an entire minute! But the minute felt like 2 or 3 minutes because of the amount of effort and strength I expended and the fatigue I felt. One of the team leaders complimented me on being able to deliver kicks and baton strikes for the entire minute. That was one of the many times I was reminded of the importance of maintaining physical fitness.

I noticed that the defensive tactics (DT) instructor was a position that could lead to other opportunities within the agency. I paid close attention during training and read the applicable manuals. Once, when the position was open, I asked to be considered for the DT instructor for my office. However, the position was given to a Hispanic male. Who said the DT instructor had to be a man?

CHAPTER 18

I'm Not Your Knight...

Finally, I made a silent vow after becoming a postal inspector that I would not get involved with another co-worker, not only in my office, but in the entire organization. However, in 2001, when I met Timothy, I reconsidered. He was assigned to another office, in another state. Timothy and I met at a retirement party weekend celebration. Although he was tall, thick, and handsome, he was not my type at all. Timothy was dark complexioned, with nice hair. He also had bowlegs. Timothy was very personable.

We met on that first night, during the informal celebration. Timothy told me that he was separated. Based on our initial conversation, I believed his separation would eventually lead to divorce. I did not think Timothy would lie about his marital status.

On the second night of the retirement party, there was a formal dinner, but not much dancing had occurred. I wore this form fitting, knee length red dress with gold plated, red jeweled accents where the spaghetti straps joined the front of the bodice. I also wore a pair of gold sandals that were popping! I felt really good about my appearance that evening. A group of us, including Timothy, decided to patronize a local night club. Since it was a chilly night, I changed into this off-white pantsuit very much suited for dancing – and dance I did! Timothy and I danced together for the remainder of the evening. When the DJ played, "I Heard it All Before," by Sunshine Anderson, that became our theme song! It was perfect for dancing.

When the weekend was over, Timothy came to my room which I shared with my friend, Valerie (Val). Val stood by watching us as we exchanged numbers. I felt that Timothy and I really had a connection. I was excited to continue communicating with him.

Shortly thereafter, Timothy was given a detail assignment in one of the western states. He invited me to visit one weekend. I had not been to that part of the country before, and I was excited to travel there. Another friend recommended that her aunt make my reservation because she had just started as a travel agent.

Timothy and I talked almost daily up until the time for the trip, nearly two months. Although we spent a lot of time on the phone, it was not enough to ease my apprehension.

While on the plane, I sat on pins and needles, full of nervous energy. When I finally arrived at my destination and deplaned, there was Timothy smiling and waiting for me. Once we were in the car, he drove me around the city giving me a short tour. At first, it looked like a rural desert, cactus and all. Eventually we approached a city-like atmosphere.

On that first evening, we went to dinner at a local restaurant. While we were sitting at the bar, a woman began talking with us. Then out of the blue, she kissed me on my cheek! Timothy thought that was the funniest thing and he teased me about it for the remainder of the weekend.

He was lodging at a two-story, corporate type rental. The units were single story and approximately 400 square feet. Each unit contained one bedroom, dining room, sitting room, and a kitchen with a breakfast bar. It was very nice and practical.

At bedtime, I was not nervous at all! I felt so relaxed with Timothy. It was obvious that Timothy was experienced at lovemaking. He was gentle and seemed to say just the right things. The next morning, when Timothy cooked breakfast, he made pancakes and the fluffiest scrambled eggs I had ever tasted!

Later that day, Timothy and I visited the local mall. That evening while enjoying the pool, I was in awe of the weather. I especially liked the warm evenings. My skin felt warm and soothing, without the discomfort of the sun rays and the sting of a sunburn. This made the pool feel like a relaxing spa. It was a wonderful day!

When Sunday morning arrived, I packed my bags and prepared to depart. Once at the airport, Timothy walked me to the ticket counter to check-in. To my chagrin, my reservation was for the following morning, and not on Sunday. The ticket agent told me that the cost would be another $200 or so to leave. Timothy did not say anything to me about staying an additional day while we were at the ticket counter. Therefore, I thought it was okay with him. Actually, I hoped it could be viewed as a nice surprise. I did not expect to be staying another day, and I told Timothy the same.

On the contrary, Timothy did not view my delay as a nice surprise. I wished he had said something before we left the airport. In hindsight, I should have hauled tail! It was unfortunate that Timothy showed me a different side of him. He mentioned the reservation faux pas at least 3 times during the remainder of the day.

The first time, he said, "We talked about this."

I responded by explaining that I had given the correct dates to my travel agent, and it was she not me who had made the mistake. I do not even remember checking the dates, but if I did, I did not notice the error. Apparently, my explanation was not enough because Timothy brought it up a second time. It was then that I realized he was insinuating that I purposely planned to stay the extra day. Why would I do that?

Timothy would not let it go and what I thought was a wonderful weekend turned sour. When it was time for dinner, we went for take-out. When I expected Timothy to give me the money to pay for the food, he rudely indicated, by motioning to me with his hand, that *I* pay for the food. I had worn out my welcome!

That night, I did not desire his touch. As we lay in bed, Timothy commented for the third time about the reservation. In response, I gritted my teeth and said, "I told you... I did not make the reservation!"

I was perturbed and my tone meant, *leave me the heck alone!* Timothy finally got the message.

When Monday morning finally arrived, I was eager to leave. I did not get much sleep after Timothy's attitude. When we arrived at the airport again, the check-in was flawless. I said good-bye with a hug and turned to walk towards my gate. When I reached the waiting area of the gate, another passenger approached me. She explained that she noticed Timothy and I part from each other. She told me that when I walked away from him, Timothy watched me until I was no longer in his sight. She added how "cute" it was. I told her, "Thank you." It was something I would never have known if she had not told me. But I found Timothy's behavior after parting from him, interesting and a little strange.

Once I returned home, we continued to communicate. I could not help but think about the first two days of the trip that seemed so perfect. Eventually, I forgave Timothy for his behavior on the third day because I should have been more considerate of his time and asked him if he had other plans for that Sunday. After all, he was on detail. I should not have assumed that it would not be an inconvenience.

Unbeknownst to me, Val told her boyfriend, Jack, that I had gone to visit Timothy while he was on detail. She knew it was not Jack's business. However, divulging my secret to Jack was her way of talking about me behind my back. Val was still a little salty because Jack had shown some interest in me while he was dating her. If I had realized she would hold Jack's behavior against me, I would have kept that little detail to myself.

As a result, Timothy called me to say that Jack called him and said, "I know Carolyn spent the weekend with you."

Timothy said that when he tried to deny it, he was told, "Man *I know...*"

Timothy asked me who I had told. When I admitted that it was Val, Timothy said, "She is not your friend."

Despite Jack and Val discussing my business, I really thought something was good between Timothy and me. I wanted to spend time with him again. When I expressed my sentiments about Timothy with my best friend, she said, "Girl, you got it bad!"

Well, whatever I had, I lost it very quickly. During one of our conversations, Timothy told me, "I'm not your knight in shining armor." Whatever I said to prompt that response from him, I do not exactly remember. I can only imagine that Timothy was responding to something I had said because I was falling for him – *fast*! I can only guess that my expectations for him were way too high.

When Timothy and I finally discussed seeing each other again, he suggested our meeting in another state. I was confused as to why another state was necessary. So, when I suggested visiting him again, Timothy's response was,

"How are you going to visit me when I have a wife and kids!"

I felt like I had been punched in my stomach! I had truly been played. The integrity of the men in my line of work was consistently selective. I could not understand how they separated having integrity from their personal lives unless it was also not present in their professional lives.

My first thought was that Timothy did not remember the lies he told me about being separated and unhappy, and how he had married the wrong person. Since when did being separated mean living at home with your wife and kids? He did, however, admit that he had kids.

I had no intention of continuing my affair with Timothy. When he called me, I pretended that I was not upset. I never encouraged any type of intimate relationship with him again. I blamed myself for being stupid enough to believe Timothy in the first place. The red flag was the invitation to visit him in a state in which he did not live. How convenient it must have been! Not to mention the fact that I may not have been the only woman who had also visited him while he was away from his wife and kids.

What was most important to me was my career aspirations within the organization. There was a possibility that I could have been required to work with him in the future. Consequently, I wanted to ensure that if that happened, what others may have seen between us would be strictly professional. I prayed and asked God to remove any desire I had for Timothy.

When I finally saw Timothy again, it was at least nine months later at the 2002 annual NOBLE Training Conference and Exhibition held in Tampa, FL. Each year the conference presented a unique training experience and hosted notable speakers. I met so many NOBLE inspectors and other law enforcement officers at those conferences throughout the years, and forged relationships that have remained strong until this day. However, NOBLE conferences were also a venue for love relationships and extra-marital affairs known and unknown by one or both parties.

As I was browsing through the exhibit hall, I ran into Timothy. Coincidentally, he was with Jack. I quickly said hello to Jack since he was staring me in my face and proceeded to speak with Timothy. I asked Timothy how he was doing and if he had brought his kids with him. I could see that they were both taken aback by my question. Timothy answered, "No, I didn't bring my kids."

Jack stared at me incredulously as I matter-of-factly spoke to Timothy. I deserved an academy award for my performance, but I was not acting. I felt no desire for Timothy. The Lord had truly answered my prayers.

I saw Timothy once more during the conference. We were at a small gathering where hors d'oeuvres were served and dancing was being held. I wore this simple, gold A-line dress, which had a slight shimmer. (It must have commanded some attention because the following day, a man approached me and asked if I was wearing the gold dress the night before!) I spoke to Timothy briefly but danced with other people. If Jack had told anyone about Timothy and me, I gave no evidence to support the allegation. However, I knew that I would suffer the consequences of my actions at some point, simply because Jack knew about us, and he gossiped like a little girl!

Periodically, during the years, Timothy called me to ask how I was. We often talked about work gossip or significant events occurring within the organization. There were several times during my career that I visited his home city for a work assignment. I had no qualms about contacting Timothy to say hello.

Once, while working in his city, Timothy and a co-worker invited me to lunch. At the lunch spot, the waitress was very rude towards me. I got the impression that she knew the wives of either Timothy or the co-worker. During another visit, I met Timothy for a non-alcoholic drink. Afterwards, we returned to my hotel and Timothy entered the lobby with me. Once I said thank you and good night, I ascended the stairway to my room. When I looked back, I could see Timothy still standing there expectantly. I politely waved goodbye.

A year or so later, I was attending a concert and met a male inspector who was new to the Inspection Service. He said Timothy had told him what a good person I was. I was somewhat surprised by this. Not that I was not a good person, but why was this even discussed? Then it occurred to me that perhaps I was this good person because I had not chased behind Timothy or made a ruckus about his lying and chasing after me. Besides, what good could have come of it if I had?

Like a Sister

Val and I were in the academy together. She was the other African American female in my class. We did not hit it off at first, but I grew to love her. I treated her like a sister.

Initially, Val reminded me of another friend I once had, so much so, that I called Val by my other friend's name. It was ironic that they were so similar in personality. Both were smart, confident women, but seemed to have something against me. Even Val told me that she did not think we would be friends. That was confirmation that my initial reservations about our budding friendship were correct.

When we graduated from the academy, we were both able to return to our home states. It was a blessing, especially since I was still married to Dan at the time. Dan had been sitting on a powder keg expecting me to be assigned to another city and state so that it could be the reason for another argument.

Dan did not like Val! It seemed that he thought she was a negative influence on me since she was single. One weekend in 1997, I rented a Toyota RAV4, and I drove with my daughter to Tampa, FL to see the Titanic Exhibit. Val met me there. She also had a child who was about the same age as my daughter. Dan behaved like we were getting together to chase men.

Val also met Jack in 1997, at our first NOBLE conference which was held in Miami, FL. She seemed to really like Jack, and he seemed to like her too. Val hosted a family picnic and invited me and my daughter. Jack was also there and attempted to have a cordial conversation with me. I felt uncomfortable speaking with him because of his awkward glances.

In 1998, NOBLE was held in New Orleans, LA. It was my first conference after my divorce. I also brought my daughter along with me because NOBLE held separate events for spouses and children. My daughter was about 16 years old at the time. She also made a couple of life-long friends while attending NOBLE.

In New Orleans, I met Reggie while attending a cocktail hour in a hotel suite. While checking things out, I felt that someone was watching me. When I looked around, my eyes met the gaze of this man. When I decided to leave the suite, I thought, *this man is going to follow me.* Sure enough, by the time I was outside of the suite, and a few feet from the door, there he was right behind me. He was holding an alcoholic drink in his hand. He said, "You are so sexy!"

In response, I said, "Is that the best you can do, or is that liquor talking for you?"

Reggie, surprised at my response, was speechless. He laughed. I laughed too and walked away from him.

The following day, during the evening event, Reggie approached me again and said, "Let me try this again."

He extended his hand to shake mine and said, "Hi, my name is Reggie. What is your name?"

I laughed, shook his hand, and said, "Carolyn. That's much better."

We laughed about our initial meeting for a long time.

Reggie worked for another agency and lived in a different state than I did. Since NOBLE was a national conference, the likelihood of meeting someone from my same state was rare. We exchanged business cards and communicated often over the next year.

In 1999, Reggie and I were both scheduled to attend the NOBLE conference in Portland, Oregon. I brought my daughter with me again. By this time, I had the biggest crush on Reggie. I was very excited to see him.

In Portland, the hotel was comprised of several buildings and the conference guests were spread out among them. Reggie and I were hanging out, having good clean fun. We actually took a selfie with one of those one-time use Kodak cameras, using the mirror in his hotel room. Apparently, Jack saw Reggie and I together at some point during the evening. I thought it may have been when Reggie walked me to my room via the long paths between the hotel buildings. I certainly did not see Jack.

Within the week following the conference, Reggie called to tell me that Jack had called him asking about me. Reggie and Jack belonged to the same fraternity and had exchanged business cards during the conference. I was a little annoyed and confused as to why Jack would question Reggie about me. Reggie said Jack asked him, "Was that Carolyn you were with in Portland?"

Reggie responded, "Yes, it was."

Reggie purposely did not provide any details to Jack, but he assured me that Jack liked me.

I said, "How could Jack like me when he is dating my friend?"

Reggie answered, "Trust me, he likes you."

I could only imagine that Jack wanted some details about my relationship with Reggie. But since Reggie actually liked and respected me, he provided Jack no details.

I thought it important to give Val a heads up about *her man*. I gave her limited details of what had transpired between Jack and Reggie, omitting Reggie's opinion about Jack liking me. Val dismissed the entire incident and seemed annoyed that I even told her. After that, I noticed that Val seemed different towards me, and she continued to see Jack. When I learned that she told Jack about my visiting Timothy while he was on a detail, a whole two years after the conversation between Jack and Reggie, I knew it was for spite.

Val and I continued to travel and attend retirement parties and other work-related functions together. Sometimes, we took short vacations and worked on our resumes. We were determined to be ready for the next promotional opportunity and increase our chances of making the shortlist for higher level job interviews.

Eventually Jack and Val discontinued seeing one another. Shortly thereafter, Val met a man through her circle of friends and eventually married him. Although Val was married, she and Jack remained friends. I did not learn until at least 10 years later that Jack was also married. But for how long was the burning question. I would have bet money that it was for the entire time Val had known him!

Whenever our agency had group trainings, Jack was sometimes in attendance too. He always gave me attitude and was consistently rude only when Val was present. It was blatantly obvious that he felt it necessary to go out of his way to prove to Val that he did not like me. Jack exhibited the kind of behavior you would expect from a child.

I am sure that whenever I expressed my thoughts to Val about Jack's behavior, she repeated whatever I said to Jack. The fact that Jack's behavior towards me was okay with Val always bothered me. But I realized that she was insecure. She never really got over the Jack and Reggie conversation years prior. Nevertheless, I continued to be her friend.

A year or so later, prior to the 2002 NOBLE conference that was held in Tampa, FL, Val's husband was killed by a drunk driver. I was devastated for her. My cousin had also passed away during the same week. It was a difficult for me to choose between attending my cousin's funeral or being with Val for her husband's arrangements and funeral. But after discussing the situation with my mother, we thought Val needed me more. One of Val's local friends also phoned me to ask when I was arriving. Her friend expressed that I was Val's closest friend. I had already scheduled annual leave for an entire week to support Val through what I thought would be a difficult time.

Consequences

In 2001, the NOBLE Conference was held in Washington DC. I used it as a vacation and one of my home girls accompanied me. It was during this conference that I believe I experienced the consequences of my affair with Timothy.

I am fully aware that in organizations of a large size, it is not unusual when there are mostly men in the workplace, that women (or men) may encounter sexist remarks or unwanted advances. But after my affair with Timothy was halted, I was speaking with two male inspectors during the conference. A higher-level male manager approached us and interjected, "I saw you last night, I recognized you from the back!"

In response, I said, "Excuse me." Very embarrassed, I removed myself from their presence.

Even before that happened, I was on personal travel and ran into one of the two males that was present when interrupted with the crass remark. We had a conversation while sitting next to each other on an airplane. In that conversation, he told me that he had *very* fulfilling relationships with two other women while being married. I thought, *how disgusting!* I was recently divorced from Dan at the time. I told him that I never had any thoughts of cheating on my spouse, even when I was not happy with him. I expressed that he could have had a good sexual relationship with his wife, if he tried. I asked him, "What can you do with another woman that you cannot also do with your wife?" The question went unanswered.

Ironically, during the 2002 NOBLE conference in Tampa, I met another inspector who justified his extramarital affairs or relationships with other women because he clearly advised women that he was married. He further stated believing the revelation would somehow quell the woman's feelings or prevent her from wanting more than a sexual romp. I exclaimed, "That's nasty!"

I told him, "You don't know how a woman is going to feel about you after sex." I further stated, "If she cares about you or likes the sex, you will have a problem whether she knows about your wife before or after the sex."

Despite my lecture, he still asked, when the elevator stopped at his floor, "You going to your room?"

Before the elevator doors closed, I said, "Yeah."

I was amazed at the rationale of those men attempting to explain or justify why they have extramarital affairs. But since those encounters happened after my affair with Timothy, I could not help but wonder if that is why I was approached. There is a slight possibility that it was just normal conversations for them, and they had no knowledge of my affair. Nevertheless, I never wanted to be known as a woman who wants to be with another woman's husband, and I did not appreciate being put in that position.

The best advice regarding men that I was ever given, was offered by a male inspector. We became acquainted after spending an entire night on surveillance for a case. One day we were talking while riding on the elevator. I cannot recall how the conversation began exactly, but I will never forget what he told me. He said, "You are a very desirable woman. You have to be careful."

It was good advice, and especially helpful in my personal life when meeting men. Although, I must admit that several times I forgot to apply the advice and made stupid decisions when I believed what I later discovered were lies!

Instant Replay

I'm Not Your Knight...

Many men use the "I'm separated" excuse when they are happily married and want to cheat. There are also many women who do not care about a man's marital status. Those same women prefer that men are married when they date them because it allows them to have the intimacy without the other work that is required of a real relationship. Consequently, I believe that Timothy really did forget what he told *me* about his marital status, and probably assumed that I did not care.

When Timothy acknowledged that he was *still* with his wife and kids, if he had ever left, that involuntary reaction that felt like a punch in my stomach was my brain dealing with the disappointment and anxiety of being played. It was another form of *purging* for me. I was absolutely done!

At the time when I met Timothy, I had just begun to explore my professional options, and I had hoped to achieve a detail assignment too! Therefore, I made a conscious decision to maintain a professional relationship. Timothy, however, maintained communication with me for several years after we had both retired.

At one point, Timothy made a statement that led me to believe that he thought I was complicit in his infidelity all those years ago. I was offended and felt compelled to set the record straight. I immediately told him, "If I had known the truth about your marital status, what happened between us would never have happened...I chose to maintain a platonic relationship with you."

It appeared to be a sore spot with Timothy because he retorted, "How do you know I did not choose to maintain one with you."

Whatever! I guess Timothy did not like that I admitted purposely controlling our interaction for all those years, and he was none the wiser. Or he just wanted to have the last word!

CHAPTER 19

He's the One!

It was on a Sunday during the month of April, in the spring of 2002, that I met George. Time sprang forward on that day, for everyone but me! I missed my plane when I arrived at the airport an hour late. The passengers had already boarded, and the cabin doors were shut. I told the ticket agent that I had to get to Maryland. How would I explain to my supervisor that I had missed my plane because I did not know that time was moving forward?

I was scheduled to attend a large volume mailer class at the postal training facility in Maryland. It was the same facility that housed me for four months in 1996 when I was in the Inspection Service academy. This time, I would be the only inspector in the class, participating incognito.

When I finally arrived in Maryland late that evening, I saw George for the first time in the lobby area. We were both looking at the posted schedule of events and realized we were in the same class. George was about 6'3 tall, light complexioned, and handsome. Even though he had broad shoulders, he was slim. His physique was much like a football player. He was plain ole fine!

We entered the elevator together and were alone. I will never forget the anxiety I felt while standing near him in the elevator. I believed he felt it too! When we arrived on the second floor, our rooms were right next to each other! We parted and said good night.

On the next day, he sat on the last chair in my row, approximately four seats behind me. The class itself was uneventful, filled with a lot of technical information. I was supposed to be incognito, but during the entire four days of class, the instructor told the participants regarding different areas of the course, "You don't want to do that, the inspectors will come after you!" It was rather obvious she knew who I was.

Each day of training, I retired to my room immediately after class to work on my resume to meet a deadline for a job vacancy. I worked until an hour or so before the cafeteria closed. It was on one of those evenings that George waited for me. He knew I had to eat. I recall standing at the soup island and his approaching me to make small talk. I said, "I'll come over there."

When I joined him at his table, we exchanged the normal platitudes. George was from the tri-state area of the United States. He was the youngest of three children and had a young son. George was a supervisor at his company. He asked me, "What have you been doing [at the post office] for 18 years?"

I answered quietly, "I wasn't going to say..."

"You aren't one of those people she's talking about!" George said quickly.

I nodded my head.

He said, "Your secret is safe with me."

I told George that I had been working on my resume for a job vacancy to explain my late arrival for dinner. I probably mentioned how competitive it was to land a job. I am not sure if it was that night or the following night, but I asked George to read a qualification statement that I had written on my resume.

When George came to my room, he looked around like there was a hidden camera. *What is he looking for?* The training facility was once a nunnery. Therefore, the rooms were small and comprised of only a bed, bathroom, and maybe a desk.

I was sitting on the bed with my laptop, wearing a long sleeved, long pant, Victoria's Secret sleeper. I turned the laptop around for George to read what I had written. When he knelt to read the qualification statement, I saw complete sincerity in his manner. My heart skipped a beat!

George, after reading the qualification statement, said everything was there and he understood it perfectly. I thought his perspective would be perfect because he knew nothing about my line of work, and that was the type of reader I was writing for. We talked a little more, and he departed to his room for the night.

The last day of training concluded right before lunch time. I was sitting with the instructor, who confirmed she knew who I was. George walked by the table and said, "Carolyn, I'm going to call you!"

I said, "Okay!"

A few days later, George introduced himself to me again through an email communication. I still have a copy of it this day. He basically said that he was a workaholic and that he and his best friend from college shared an apartment. I was so anxious for George's call to come. When he finally called, I fumbled with the phone and disconnected it. When we finally spoke, I hesitated because I thought he was this other guy who had the same last name. Then I heard him say, "It's George Jones."

George and I talked for about three months over the phone, getting to know each other. Soon we began discussing his visiting South Florida along with several of his friends. None of them had been to Florida before. But when it was time to secure a reservation, it was only George who would come.

He arrived in July, the day after the 2002 NOBLE conference ended in Tampa. I am sure I anticipated George's visit the entire time I was at NOBLE. By this time, my daughter was in her second year of college. George stayed with me 3 days and 2 nights.

I was just around the corner from the Ft Lauderdale, FL airport when George called to say he was waiting for me on the curb. I reassured him that I was on my way. When I picked him up, we went to Dania Beach for dinner at a seafood restaurant that I had made reservations for in advance. At the restaurant, there was a Louis Armstrong song playing. George actually knew the lyrics and sang them to me. I thought of how different his upbringing must have been from mine. The only Armstrong song I knew was "What a Wonderful World."

Since I was born in Miami and grew up during the 60's and early 70's, the popular songs were a mixture of music played on the radio station Y-100. It was not until the late 70's that I was introduced to the R&B and blue-eyed soul music playing on the radio station WEDR. Armstrong was not played on those stations. But I knew my father's favorite song was "Patches," sung by Clarence Carter. My mother often claimed that country music was a part of her upbringing since she was born in Knoxville, TN. My siblings and I laughed at that. Therefore, I found it very interesting that George knew the lyrics of a different Armstrong song.

After dinner, we walked on the beach, which was just across the street from the restaurant. In South Florida, the beach is to the east of Interstate 95. There are many hotels and restaurants on, or across the street from, the beach. George held my hand as we walked along the beach. My hand seemed so small while being held by his. Then George turned to me and spontaneously planted his lips on mine and kissed me. Then he said, "How could I not do that," referring to the perfect setting of the beach at sunset for our first kiss.

When we returned to my house, George gave me the Cliff Notes version of his family background. He had already told me about his two siblings, who lived in different parts of the United States. George continued by verbally introducing me to his son's mother, Trina, and gave me the background of their relationship. But when George talked about his parents, I sensed something about his family dynamics. I asked him, "Are they going to accept you having a relationship?"

George said confidently, "They won't have a choice!"

When we retired for bed, we laid there for a moment before I touched his shoulder and motioned to him that it was okay to touch me. During sex, he was gentle and even polite. It was an absolutely perfect ending to a good day.

The next day George cut my grass. Then somehow in the middle of the day, we ended up in bed again. Later that evening we tried to enjoy the pool, but strangely, the water was too chilly. Once we dried off, we ended up in the bed a second time!

The next morning, we went to church – I know what you are thinking! Afterwards we picked up some food and drove to the airport. When he left, I thought, *he's the one!*

So, our relationship began. On our next visit, I flew to his home state. We stayed in a hotel located in the downtown area. He took me on my first horse and carriage ride, and we toured the historical sites. What was most memorable on the tour was seeing the extremely tall and old buildings. I enjoyed sight-seeing with George immensely.

George had planned for me to meet his parents, but when we arrived at their home, they had pulled a disappearing act. George seemed genuinely bewildered as to why they were not home. But I knew it was on purpose. They were showing George (and me) that they were not accepting his having someone special in his life, let alone a relationship. Reluctantly, I realized that I had foretold this situation. But this was only the beginning. What followed were a chain of events that were characterized by a string of never-ending manipulation, and George was the victim.

First, a party had been planned for George's son, but George was not told about it until after he had made reservations to visit me. Even though George apologized for not being available, it caused a big disagreement between George and Trina. What happened next? Trina relinquished custody of their son and dropped him off at George's parents' house for a permanent visit. Then George decided it was better to move back home with his parents because his son was so young, and he worked long hours. Although it seemed a viable solution, it eliminated any independence George would have.

George and I managed to keep our relationship together despite the manipulation occurring around him. Our feelings for each other were growing and I knew I was falling in love with him. Since George was living at home with his parents, I had spoken with his mother once or twice. She was very pleasant over the phone and seemed to like me.

In 2003, I sold my home to be flexible for a quick relocation in case I got one of the jobs I had been applying for. My contingency plan was to voluntarily transfer to Georgia, an area that I believed would support my career endeavors. So, I moved in with my mother and stepfather, believing it would be of short duration.

During another visit with me, I took George to a function hosted by my church. It was at that event that George met my mother. My mother pulled George aside and began talking with him. I was curious and wanted to eavesdrop, but I knew my mother was probably inspired to talk with George. When I asked him about their conversation later, he said my mother told him about her background and upbringing.

George had begun to work extra-long hours and even some weekends. It was hard to get him to take a break. But when he visited me again, I found some super-saver hotel deals on South Beach and Miami Beach. That time, George visited me for 5 or 6 days. We had a blast!

George

An entire year had transpired, and no job had been awarded to me. The transfer was taking longer than expected. So, in 2004, I decided to buy a townhome, something I could lease later. As soon as I paid my earnest money, the transfer came through. Faced with the decision of losing my earnest money and moving to Georgia, or staying and purchasing the townhome, I purchased the townhome instead.

George and I had begun to yearn for each other, and it seemed that we needed to make some important decisions. I sensed that George wanted to come to Miami when the townhome was purchased, but I would not shack-up with another man again without being married. I was prepared to talk with George about my stance if that is what he was thinking. But George had begun making decisions on his own. Soon I received a phone call from George. He had been arguing with his mother. George said he told his mother that he wanted to move to Miami to be with me and my mother. *Oh my God!*

His mother was terribly angry and asked him, "Do you expect me to raise your son?"

I knew George was thinking something, but I did not expect that! George asked me what I thought about the situation. Although it pained me, I said, "I think you should stay."

I knew his son needed him. If George had considered a marriage with me, the conversation would have been different.

I knew this would not have gone over well with George's mother. I also knew that she probably blamed me for George's thought process. The next time I phoned to speak with George, his mother answered and was extremely rude towards me – giving me deafening silence in between the few words she had spoken. I was shocked that I could feel her disdain for me through the phone. The damage was done! I did not call her house for a long time after that. My feelings were extremely hurt, and I told George about his mother's behavior. He said, "I believe you."

It seemed that maybe George had begun to think about marriage. He had planned at least two trips to visit me, but they never happened. George finally told me, "I'm sending for you."

This is serious, I thought. But I was ready.

When he did not send for me, I scheduled a trip instead. By the time I arrived to see George, he appeared extremely tired and confused. The next sign of manipulation I witnessed was when George said how concerned he was about introducing another woman into his son's life. I knew that was his mother talking. Then he told me, "...you're not ready to get married again."

But George had not asked me to get married. He just seemed to be making a statement.

I told him, "George, your mother wants to choose your wife for you."

"How can she do that?" That was all he said.

I knew our relationship had taken a big hit. George was trying to come into his manhood and his mother was consistently knocking him back with negative ideas. George had tremendous respect for his mother, and she used that.

I was so disappointed, but I tried to keep us together. When I left him that weekend, I knew that there was no rebounding from there. Our relationship really struggled the following year, and there was nothing I could do. I was on the outside looking in, watching what was happening around George.

George took a second job, and his time was even more restricted. It was on a night that he was working at the second job, while we were talking on the phone, that he said, "I love you... I care for you, but I need to be here for my son."

I said, "I love you, too! ...and I understand."

I often spoke with my friend Leila, who I have known since I was 16 years old. She was almost 20 years my senior and like a second mother to me. When I told Leila what was happening between George and me, she said, "He just wants his mother to give him her support, but she won't give it to him."

That was exactly right, I thought. But I knew that before we started.

Instant Replay

George

By 2005, I was still trying to remind George of what we had. When he told me about a wedding that he was attending in Montgomery, I arranged my schedule so that I could meet him there. But that was not the first time that I had arranged my schedule to see George. Since I traveled for work often, I had seen George a few times at the end of an assignment.

I understood what it was to be a single parent, and I supported George. Therefore, I put no pressure on him about marriage. I just wanted us to maintain a relationship.

The weekend in Montgomery was fabulous! We got so much attention that George received phone calls from fraternity brothers asking, "Where did you meet her?" But I was truly in love with George. Why could he not see that?

CHAPTER 20

Just Another Detail

After about six years as a postal inspector, I decided that I wanted more responsibility and began applying for higher-level positions, but I did not want to supervise inspectors. I had worked with enough inspectors and supervising them directly was not desirable. Program managers were higher-level postal inspectors with non-supervisory duties, a much more appealing position. Most program managers were located at headquarters in Washington DC, an area in which I wanted to relocate.

I learned to write about my investigative experiences succinctly, enabling me to compete and obtain several interviews for program manager positions. However, after being interviewed each time, if I was one of the top three candidates, I was not offered the position. I also applied for an internal affairs position, which was also located at headquarters. Strangely enough, I was notified about achieving the short-list for that position. The lead interviewer commented that if he was the selecting official, he would have promoted me.

Also in 2003, I was interviewed for a program manager position and earned a four-week detail at headquarters. The selecting official offered me the detail. I had a glimmer of hope that I made a favorable impression, and it would become a permanent position – but it did not. The position was awarded to the inspector who had been detailed in the position prior to me and for much longer than I was. Although I appreciated being given the opportunity, I believed the selecting official was just patronizing me. I remembered a conversation with him during which he encouraged me to achieve other certifications (i.e., fraud examiner, public accountant, auditor) to become more competitive. It was condescending advice since the prerequisite for most program manager positions did not require anything other than being an inspector and specific investigative knowledge, skills, and abilities. Suggesting that I achieve additional qualifications outside of what were required for the actual job position only confirmed that unwritten qualifications were being used to promote individuals.

I never imagined that I would desire to compete for higher level positions while in the field of investigations. I should have been satisfied, but I was inspired to do more. I experienced first-hand the difficulty of entering a male-dominated career field and what it meant regarding competition for higher-level positions and promotional opportunities. I often asked for feedback to help improve my interview skills. Once, I was told that my answers were not succinct. I thought, *what?* The response was entirely subjective and not the constructive feedback that I expected. It was déjà vu.

Sexy Cases

I decided to defect from the Inspection Service and apply for a vacancy with the Postal IG located at their headquarters. "Defect" was the term coined when inspectors decided to leave the Inspection Service and enter its rival, the Postal IG. But there was an application process. I was so sure the Postal IG would have been a great fit for me. I knew that very few candidates could offer my postal knowledge or background. I never doubted that I would receive an interview. However, during the interview I got the impression that there was bias towards me. This impression was confirmed when one of my answers was challenged by one of the interviewers.

In response to one of the questions, I relayed:

> During a task force briefing for a robbery investigation, we were told a chain link fence had been cut. When no one was assigned to physically surveil the area close to the fence, I suggested that someone be assigned there. In response, the task force leader stated that the intel did not suggest that the fence would be an access point. On the day of surveillance, one of the perpetrators tried to get through the fence, but he was too fat! As my partner and I sat in the law enforcement vehicle listening to the audio-visual surveillance, he said, "They are doing just what you said they would." I responded,

"Uh huh!" That blunder must have spooked all the perpetrators because the robbery did not occur on that day. No one was physically assigned to the area close to the chain link fence to stop the fat guy if he had gotten through.

After giving the three interviewers a full account of what happened, one of them told me that I did not put forth enough effort to convince the task force leader about the viable access point. *Oh my God! What more could I have said?* When I inquired later as to why I was not offered the position, I learned the interviewers thought I should have applied for an entry level investigator position. It was an insult! An entry level Postal IG position would have been a downgrade in pay in comparison to my Inspection Service position. Not to mention that my background and experience was way above entry level and surely above any of my interviewers. It was then that I knew there were inherent issues between the Postal IG and the Inspection Service.

By this time, Mary (my mentor) had moved on to become second in command, assistant inspector in charge (AIC) and later an INC in two other areas of the United States. Mary often provided encouragement regarding my promotional endeavors. She even spoke with Manny (my AIC) on my behalf, hoping to get his support for my promotional endeavors. After a series of interviews, it was disappointingly obvious that Manny was not giving me "the nod." I knew that if Manny had taken the initiative to offer favorable feedback to some of the selecting officials I encountered along the way, I may have had some success getting promoted. Once I understood that I did not have Manny's full support while on my path, all my promotional endeavors were in vain.

Soon after, Manny called me to his office and advised that he was changing my assignment to investigate prohibitive mailings which meant investigating those who used the mail to move illegal narcotics and child pornography. He said the new assignment would give me the criminal investigative experience I needed to help me with my promotional endeavors. *Finally!* Eventually, I made one of the biggest cocaine seizures the office had had in a long time. I also made three arrests related to that case. I gained some fame in the office for a while and was congratulated by some of the male inspectors. In reflection, it was the most fun I had had in my entire career!

I also arrested a child pornography offender. As a matter of fact, my second appearance on the news was after executing a search warrant at the home of a second child pornography offender. Child pornography cases were no fun! As the case agent, I had to review the videos and other printed materials confiscated to disclose if any underage children were featured. Those are vivid memories that will never go away!

While investigating prohibitive mailings, I had another well-documented narcotics and money laundering case that was not prosecuted. The suspect resided in the United States, but his co-conspirators resided in the US Virgin Islands. I was assigned the case after a drug interdiction where a canine alerted to a package. Initially, I was referred to a District of Columbia prosecutor who subsequently referred the case to a US Virgin Islands prosecutor. She explained there was an initiative targeting those specific cases. I was so excited! It was my first time traveling to a US territory for a case. I was convinced that the case would be a priority there. Once I arrived to present the case in person, the prosecutor brushed me off! Her brusque and impatient nature gave me the impression that she somehow knew my suspect; or resented my encroaching on her territory to bring a case against Virgin Island citizens. It was incredibly difficult to believe I traveled all that way to be snubbed. With her apparent disposition, I could not justify wasting the Inspection Service's money extending my stay for another day hoping to convince her to take the case. I returned home the following day with nothing to report for my hard work.

Eventually, I had quite a few "sexy cases" on my resume – that is what the guys called interesting and *newsworthy* cases. I was sure that including those sexy cases on my resume would have given me the recognition needed to be taken seriously and awarded me that long-awaited promotion – but they did not. Even though my AIC reassigned me to work criminal cases, I did not inquire again about any special assignments or promotions in my current office. I had observed too many times that the White and Hispanic males were the favorites and given all the opportunities. Therefore, I focused my efforts on getting out of that office!

Through networking, I learned that INCs from other areas often suggested applying for details in other states to increase one's chances for promotion. My only interest was to relocate to headquarters and become a program manager. Therefore, I concentrated my efforts on applying only for positions that I desired. I was not willing to apply for just any position hoping to get promoted and I stunted my growth because of it.

Moving On

In early 2005, I had had enough and decided to defect from the Inspection Service again. The Postal IG opened a local office and I applied. This time, I had more investigative experience than I had when I applied for the Postal IG some years prior. As the hiring process progressed, I was approached by at least two inspectors who said they *heard* I had applied for the Postal IG. I often wondered why there was no level of confidentiality within the Postal Service. I mentioned to Mary about those inquiries from inspectors about my Postal IG application, and she advised that I speak with my INC before he *heard* it from someone else.

I went to see my INC. In the past, he was always supportive and even excited when I would get interviews, a stark contrast to Manny (my AIC) from whom I needed the nod. It was obvious my AIC had more influence than my INC. As a matter of fact, my INC was a former audit executive – go figure! (The Inspection Service appeared to favor criminal investigations over audit investigations.) After the formalities, I told my INC, "It is obvious that I am not the type of person that the agency wants to promote." I continued, admitting that I was being hired by the Postal IG. He thanked me for my candor. When my AIC learned that I had spoken with the INC about leaving the Inspection Service, he told me it was "classy." He further stated that I could always come back if I wanted to. I still wonder if I should have taken him up on that offer. But my mother always said, "You don't go back!" So, I kept moving forward.

In February 2005, at my going away luncheon, I unexpectedly became emotional. Although I was excited to start anew, the tears seemed to flow out of nowhere. I did not share the negative sentiments that most inspectors had about transferring from the Inspection Service to the Postal IG – we all worked for the Postal Service. Why was I crying?

Instant Replay

Transitioning from the Postal Service to the Inspection Service was the coup de grâce – icing on the cake, for most postal employees. The Inspection Service was the elite level of the Postal Service. Achieving that level was something to be proud of. For women, it broke the glass ceiling – the invisible barrier through which better jobs can be seen yet unattained for those who wanted career advancement, especially because law enforcement is a male dominated career.

Seeing Larry almost 12 years later was an opportunity to confront some of my vomit from the past. Although he blocked me from moving forward at such an early stage of my career, it was a vivid reminder that I did not allow him to thwart my drive and determination to achieve a higher-level position.

Those eight years as a postal inspector shaped and molded me both personally and professionally. Personally, working with a bunch of men, who were most times the primary bread winners for their families, made me keenly aware of the importance of preparing for retirement. Their conversations were often about contributing to the Thrift Savings Plan (401k) and making sound investments – and I listened! Professionally, I gained realistic expectations regarding my promotional endeavors, but I did not quit! I also developed resilience when I competed and failed, always believing in my abilities regardless of the disappointments I experienced. Not to mention that my use of profanity increased exponentially as I creatively combined expletives to express my sentiments about those same disappointments and disparate treatment!

In hindsight, I am sure both prosecutors knew the importance of accepting my cases and what a successful prosecution would have done for my reputation and career as an investigator. I believe that if they had been men or I had been a man, those arrest warrants would have been issued. Since I did not have a personal relationship with either prosecutor, their inaction led me to believe it was a professional bias that I would never be privy to. I am sure if I had reported the prosecutors to their managers, I would have risked being shunned by other prosecutors for my future cases. However, for the remainder of my career, there were other male and female prosecutors who gladly accepted my well-documented cases.

In 2005, I learned that I was not the only African American female postal inspector who had been unsuccessful in getting a promotion. There were several other African American females who had been overlooked or bypassed for higher-level positions during a specific timeframe. Management spear-headed only certain people for higher-level positions. I was kept in what was thought to be "my place." It was bittersweet to learn a year later that my promotional efforts and experiences were shared by several other African American females. Consequently, a class action lawsuit was filed against the Inspection Service.

I was invited to join the class action. As a result, I provided a chronology of my application experiences, which enabled me to effectively contribute to the success of the class action. I also supplied at least one or two resumes to represent the many qualified applicants of that group. I was contacted again in 2013, for additional documentation. The class action lawsuit concluded in 2015. Specific plaintiffs, including myself, were awarded a monetary settlement. Poetic justice again!

I *recognized* that even after demonstrating the knowledge, skills, and abilities to be promoted, it was never enough to be given a promotion or an opportunity for greater responsibility. I constantly *prepared* myself for that next position. I remained abreast of the vacancy announcements and always kept my resume updated for quick completion to meet submission deadlines. My investigative abilities were the same whether my cases were prosecuted or not; therefore, I continued applying for promotional opportunities. Very few, if any, interviewers asked about the prosecutorial resolutions of my cases. However, I never regretted applying for only positions that I desired, regardless of stunting my growth. Why not? Because I remembered that adage, "Don't apply for a job that you don't want, you just may get it!"

I finally accepted defeat when I made the decision to defect from the Inspection Service. I was ready for the transition. But when I cried at my farewell luncheon, I was confused. What I did not realize until sometime later was that my spirit not only *purged* certain people from my life, but it also *purged* experiences. My spirit had shown me several times before that it has a mind of its own, purging to move on or forward to the next phase of my life. The next phase of my life was the Postal IG and what a painful adventure it was!

Part V – The Fourth Quarter

CHAPTER 21

Double Defect

I was pleased that the local Postal IG manager, whose title was assistant special agent in charge (ASAC), appreciated the experience I brought with me – that is for the entire four months that I was in his office. Four months after my arrival in the Postal IG, Mary also defected from the Inspection Service and accepted a position with the Postal IG. Mary then offered me a promotion in her office located in Atlanta, GA. When I accepted, I knew my ASAC was not happy about it. Frankly, the local agents in my new office spoke negatively about my achieving a promotion and leaving so soon after I arrived. They even rumored that Mary and I were gay, which did not surprise me since several of the agents were gay. I found it interesting that when people of color promoted people of their own race, it was often scrutinized so much more than when it happened within the *good-old-boy* network. People assumed that because Mary and I had a good work history in the Inspection Service, that she would show me favoritism. Quite the contrary, she expected nothing but the best from me. As a result, I worked even harder.

Even though I defected from the Inspection Service, I had great respect and love for it as an organization. I was told that other Postal IG agents often commented that I was quick to say I was a former inspector, as if that was all I had to be proud of. True enough, I worked hard to become an inspector and I *could* claim it with unchallenged integrity – and I did!

In retrospect, I observed that several Postal IG agents possessed a modicum of jealousy regarding inspectors. In comparison, the Inspection Service was a much more professional organization than the Postal IG. I attributed this vast difference to the "melting pot" of agents from varying IG offices, which constituted the Postal IG. Many IG agents often agency-hopped, leaving one IG for another IG. Since the Inspection Service had its own training academy, each inspector was given the same basic training and thereby possessed a common loyalty or tie that bound them together. The Postal IG agents had various backgrounds and training with no real common loyalty or ties – evidenced by the agency hopping. My history in the Postal Service and my training through the Inspection Service academy, caused me to miss that Inspection Service bond tremendously.

As fate would have it, in 2006, Mary became the manager of four states, which included my former office! There was so much in-fighting and resistance, that the offices were difficult to merge. Then, like whiplash, the Postal IG acquired two of the largest investigative functions from the Inspection Service – internal crimes and workers' compensation fraud (crimes committed by postal employees), further damaging the fragile and competitive relationship between the two Postal Service law enforcement agencies. It was unbelievable! The Inspection Service is one of the oldest law enforcement agencies in the United States, dating back to 1772 when Benjamin Franklin was Postmaster General. The Postal IG was Johnny-come-lately but had gumption!

CHAPTER 22

Star-crossed?

"Star-crossed" or "star-crossed lovers" is a phrase describing a pair of lovers whose relationship is often thwarted by outside forces. The term encompasses other meanings, but originally means the pairing is being "thwarted by a malign star" or that the stars are working against the relationship. (Wikipedia 2021)

Star-crossed - not favored by the stars: ILL-FATED (Merriam-Webster Dictionary 2021)

I had two opportunities to leave George. Remember when I said Todd called me after he and his girlfriend had broken up and I was seeing someone? Well, that someone was George. Because Todd had broken my heart, I did not want to leave George for him.

I still had the biggest crush on Reggie. We seemed perfect for each other, and our career paths were the same. Reggie and I attempted to begin a relationship after the 1999 NOBLE conference.

First, when he visited me, I was not sure what we were doing. Reggie displayed good manners and I loved the way he spoke to my daughter. But when I visited him, although we had a great time, he seemed apprehensive about us, and therefore, we were never intimate.

Shortly after my visit with him, Reggie stopped returning my calls. I had called him two or three times and left messages. When I did not hear from him, I was extremely disappointed, but there was nothing I could do. A couple of months passed; Reggie began calling me again as if nothing had happened. By that time, although my disappointment had subsided, and I did not trust him anymore.

Reggie finally offered some sort of explanation as to why he stopped calling me. He said the distance between us was an issue for him. Reggie also said that he did not want either of us to relocate for the other. He had done that for someone before, and it did not end well.

Coincidentally, or not, while I was with George, Reggie told me that he was lonely. If you recall, Danny told me he was lonely too. After hearing this string of words again, I should have recognized that Reggie was serious. My feelings were still a little hurt because he seemed indecisive about us. Nevertheless, I was genuinely torn about leaving George for Reggie. In view of my indecision, I resolved to stay with George because I still believed in him.

What We Had

After that fabulous weekend at the wedding in Montgomery, George and I managed to continue seeing each other. It was difficult because he continued to show that he was indeed the workaholic that he told me he was when I first met him. I was not a priority at times when I felt I should have been.

It was the wedding we attended before the Montgomery wedding that bonded us. One of my co-workers married and invited me to his wedding. The wedding was held in New York, and I invited George to accompany me. George said he did not sleep at all that night. I slept like a baby. Sex for us had truly evolved into lovemaking and we fit like a glove. When we made love that night, our climax involved an orgasm that seemed to linger long after it began, which I am sure accounted for my deep sleep. It was absolutely amazing!

I believed George was up all night because he really did not know what to do about us. He had mentioned several times that financially he could not do for me what he believed he should. I could not understand his reasoning. I worked and he worked. It was never important that I made more money than he did. I felt that as long as we were together, we would be fine. But George did not see it that way.

Soon after the Montgomery wedding, I relocated to Atlanta. I thought that George would have offered to help me move. But George constantly used his work as an excuse for cancelling several planned trips to visit me as well as other events, including helping me to move. But I desperately tried to keep us together.

During my first few months in Atlanta, George visited me. I lived in an investment property that I purchased on a whim. Since I had not leased it to anyone, it provided a quick transition once I got the job.

George was always helpful around the house. We painted the pickets and posts of the country porch with white paint. George also assisted me with choosing colors and paint for my new home, which was scheduled for completion a few months later. He was great with color coordination.

Once I moved into the new home, George and I were still maintaining our relationship. In early 2008, I scheduled a trip to Jamaica with a friend who cancelled on me. To my surprise, George stepped in and paid the fees for the lodging that she would have paid. It was great to have a real vacation with George again.

George finally visited me at the new home, and he was able to see the results of the chosen color palette in person. I did not know it then, but it would be the last time he would visit me while I lived in Atlanta. He scheduled another flight but cancelled it at the last minute. At one point, I attended a training that was only an hour's drive from George's home. But again, George said he could not meet me because of a work deadline. In the three years I lived in Atlanta, George visited me an average of once each year.

George claimed money was his excuse for not visiting me more often – he did not have any. He often talked about his goal to make a six-figure salary, and that goal motivated him to work as he did. Although the frequency of our visits was not enough for me, I treasured our time together more. There were a few times that I may have considered if George were seeing someone else, but I knew that he would not find again what we had. That is what motivated me!

Instant Replay

What We Had

George and I were doomed from the start. My spirit warned me that George's family would not accept his having a relationship. However, I believed George when he said, "They won't have a choice." He seemed so strong in the beginning.

When Trina made that strategic move and left their son with George's parents; and then George's mother began her manipulative tactics, the ripple effects permanently thwarted our relationship. But no matter what happened, I believed George would fight for us, and most importantly stand up for me. I thought he was strong enough to control the people and situations in his life, but either he never was or chose not to.

To make matters worse, while I was catastrophically devoted to George, Reggie found someone else to be with and married her. I believe you only get one soulmate – "*a person with whom one has a feeling of deep or natural affinity.*" (Wikipedia 2021) Reggie was mine.

CHAPTER 23

Jealousy

In 2008, Mary had an ASAC position available within my home state of Florida, in the Tampa office. I applied, competed, and made the top three. Just like that, I earned a promotion to a supervisory position within the Postal IG! Once again there was criticism about my promotion. I soon learned that the criticism was more jealousy about the actual title or position and that jealousy was shared by many. For the next five years, I worked in my new office, supervising a capable team of individuals who were resistant to my authority.

The agents were disrespectful from the very beginning. It appeared to be a combination of not wanting a manager on site and believing they were above the postal employees they investigated. It was a back-handed slap that I knew was directed towards me, my background, and experience. As a result, they purposefully demonstrated their lack of respect for me and the ASAC position.

As I jumped into managing the agents, their attitudes and behaviors were like crabs in a barrel. But instead of pulling each other down, they tried pulling me down, often misunderstanding and underestimating me. One day, one of my team members told me, "There is strength in numbers." I understood the implications of her cryptic message. However, I not only recognized their tactics, but my recognition was constantly reinforced as I was kept abreast of what they were saying about me. I learned that team member Steve verbalized that I was not smart enough to be his supervisor. Remember, there was no confidentiality in the Postal Service! Hearing about their comments second-hand, constantly reminded me of the agents' lack of professionalism.

Notwithstanding my team members' negative attitudes towards me, I persisted in attempts to boost the team's morale. I tried team-building exercises, working lunches, and one-on-one conferences, but nothing worked. Each of my strides towards promoting positive attitudes and effective communication garnered negativity and complaints. They had a plan – sabotage!

I expressed to Mary that I believed they planned to do a work stoppage as a show of defiance towards me as their supervisor. Mary replied that they would only be hurting themselves at merit time. Many days, I wanted to return to my former position and office – a place I had begun referring to as my haven. However, I knew that Mary depended on me to manage the agents and I vowed to myself that I would, no matter what happened. I was dedicated! It felt good to have management's support, but the support did not last.

Backstabber

Who was leading the mutiny? Val! After Mary and I defected, Val told me she wanted to defect too! Being the good friend that I was, I gave her a referral. Since I was well respected by the former manager, my referral was valued. Val was a good investigator; therefore, I was not embellishing just because she was a friend. Shortly thereafter, Val resigned from the Inspection Service and was hired just in the nick of time, right before the former management was dissolved.

Several months later, the current ASAC in Val's office left for another IG. Remember, the IG hopping that many people did? Mary asked if Val was interested in the ASAC position. When I asked Val, she said, *no*. Therefore, Mary used the local agents to act in the position until an ASAC could be hired. When I was hired for the ASAC position a year later, Val seemed genuinely happy for me. When Val and I talked, she was anxious for me to arrive. I had visions of our hanging out again, like we had so many times in the previous years.

It seemed like only a few weeks after I arrived that I noticed Val acting strangely towards me. When I mentioned socializing, Val told me to use the local newspapers, magazines, or the internet to learn about current events. It was obvious that I was excluded from her inner circle of friends where I was previously welcomed.

Another time, I called her on the weekend and suggested that we meet for lunch. She told me, "I've already eaten." *Whoa!* I never called her on a personal level again.

Also, during those first few weeks, I attempted to observe the agents under my supervision. Incidentally, there were nine agents assigned to me. Four, including Val, were in my office. The remaining five agents were assigned to another office located approximately 90 minutes away. On paper, they all appeared productive.

As time progressed, it appeared that the five remote agents were the more mature group, but I was not in the office with them. Employees, and in this case agents, typically did not want to be in the same office as his or her manager. However, if an individual does their job with the utmost integrity, it should not matter if they are in the same office as their manager.

Val touted that I was blessed because I had a good team. That remained to be seen. Although it was not unusual for agents to work in the field or even from home, once or twice a week, there was a process for notification. One day, Val was the only agent in the office. The others did not come in and I had no idea where they were!

I attempted to build a one-on-one relationship with each agent, hoping to build trust and mutual understanding. But my efforts were neither appreciated nor received as intended. I was accused of micro-management which was very much necessary due to their lack of respect for me and the position. I was accountable for them and their actions; therefore, I needed to learn about each of them and their work ethic. What I had witnessed up until that juncture was not their best.

Then the agents began to complain to Val about me – she had been elected their mediator. She enjoyed this power position! Val appeared to want to manage the team through me. When she pleaded their causes, Val was obviously on their side. I was always wrong. At some point Val told me, "I don't want to see you crash and burn!" Why did I have to be crashing and burning? They were crying wolf and manipulating her because they believed she had access to me. Why did Val not see that?

Several people told me Val was jealous. There may have been some truth to that. But she was asked if she had interest in the ASAC position way before I had even thought about it.

One of my last resorts was the team building exercises, which were coupled with working lunches. Val told me that the exercises were not working with the team. How could they work when it was crystal clear they had made a pact to be uncooperative? I was positive that the plan was to undermine my authority and make me look incompetent.

What was most interesting was the cryptic gift Val presented to me shortly after I arrived in Tampa. The gift was a book written by the retired four-star general Colin Powell entitled *The Leadership Secrets of Colin Powell*. I thought it a bit much to compare the agents with the caliber of people that Colin Powell would have managed. In my opinion, *All I Really Need to Know I Learned in Kindergarten* by Robert Fulghum, would have been the better titled book to describe the maturity level of the team. Although there was a reference in the book about being kind to one another, the team was obviously excluding me from any expression of kindness. However, the simplest solution was that they do their jobs and manage their cases!

I learned that Val told someone, "I don't like her!" I felt like I was punched in my stomach (again). I called my mom and told her what was happening between Val and me. My mom said, "She knows you. She knows what buttons to push!" I had to agree because too many times I wanted to curse at them. What stopped me from cursing was the promise I made to God that I would stop using profanity. It was that promise which kept me grounded and helped me hold my tongue! But most importantly, I did not want to say anything that could be misconstrued and used against me.

One of the agents from the remote office told me often that my memory was like a steel trap. My memory was something I was immensely proud of. Once Val shared something with me that I believed personal in nature. It just so happened that I was reminded of what she said. When I mentioned it to Val, we were in my office alone. She denied saying it. Val said, "I'm not trying to be funny, but I didn't tell you that!" I was dumbfounded because I did not make it up. Why did she lie? Then during a team meeting, Val repeated something personal that I had shared with her years prior regarding my personal management journey. Even old or former friends should have a code of conduct. But Val showed no honor among friends!

I was done with Val, and she knew it. I recall the day she came into my office and expressed being upset about the state of our friendship. Then she began to cry. I thought it a slight possibility that they were crocodile tears, but we were awfully close. I am sure she felt some level of pain. Even though I mechanically said, "I'm sorry I upset you," it was her fault. Our friendship would never revert to the way we were. Did Val not know that I was fully aware that she had been talking about me?

Soon my immediate supervisor visited our office, and the team bombarded him with all kinds of complaints. When my supervisor told me what the complaints were, I told him, "They are lying!"

His response? "It's a witch hunt!"

It was indeed a set up. Amid all the backstabbing and plotting, Val told my supervisor that she owed me an apology. But that apology never came.

When my brother died in 2009, Val called me to say she had a dream about me "crying violently." I assured her that I was fine. Then sometime later, I was in the office and Val told me she had the same or similar dream again. At that moment I thought, *the Spirit (of the Lord) is really riding her.* I knew she was having the dreams because of the way she had treated me. It was obvious that she was deeply bothered by the dreams, but I had adjusted to our rift. Val had not.

Val worked in my office for about two and half to three years. When she retired prematurely, as her manager, I attempted to arrange a farewell team lunch. She declined, giving the impression that she did not want to make a big deal out of retiring. It was not until someone, who assumed I was involved in the planning, contacted me to ask about her retirement luncheon that I learned about the event. I was even more disappointed that she felt it necessary to shun me. But I knew her behavior ran much deeper – it was still about her insecurities.

I also found it quite interesting that not one agent under my supervision mentioned the luncheon, indicative of their concerted effort to keep me in the dark about the event. Therefore, I pretended that I did not know about the luncheon. I surely did not want to be a party crasher!

When I received Val's farewell thank you letter and law enforcement badge plaque from headquarters, it was my opportunity to let her know I was fully aware of her antics. I said, "Here is your plaque from headquarters. You can get someone to present it to you at your luncheon."

Val was quiet. Under normal circumstances, someone from management would have presented the plaque to her. But since Val had made the event such a secret, it appeared that no one from management attended.

Val's last day finally arrived. When she came into my office to submit her final paperwork, keys, and other items, the remaining three teammates stood around my office doorway as if they were preparing to see a show.

I simply said, "I wish you well."

"Oh, I'll be fine," was her smug reply.

That was the last time I saw or spoke to Val.

Instant Replay

Backstabber

I purposely held my tongue with Val and struggled to remain professional. I wished that I could have overlooked the backstabbing or that it had never happened, especially when I reminisced about the old times. Val and I had shared what I thought was a great friendship. Her own idiosyncrasies regarding our friendship and inability to separate our work from that friendship ruined it. When my brain dealt with the *vomit* of disappointment, that involuntary reaction that felt like a punch in my stomach, I knew she was another experience that I was *purging*. My mind, body, and soul were done!

CHAPTER 24

The End?

When I moved back to Florida after I was promoted in 2008, it had been almost six years since I met George. There was no doubt in my mind that it was fate that our paths crossed. I surely thought that we would have been engaged or married by that time. I still had hope for us when George visited me shortly after I returned to Florida.

Sadly, sometime in 2009, George's father left his mother. He handled his father's disappearance remarkably well. I guess he saw it coming. Shortly thereafter, George's employer downsized and laid off its management employees. I did not think our relationship was strong enough to sustain these life-changing events. After losing his job, George received a severance package which helped him financially. Somehow, we maintained our relationship for two more years. I made an effort to see George whenever I traveled for work and was close to his city.

George had begun applying for other jobs. By 2011, he had 2-3 strong prospects. I will never forget George's phone call in 2011. He said that he wanted us to make a two-year plan. George had received a second interview for a job, and he said, "If I get this job, things are going to change for us!"

"Okay!" I was so happy for George (and us).

I knew George had worked hard to get to that second interview. But he was not offered the job. It was then that we discussed relocation to Florida again. George's son was in college, and he was ready to job hunt the old-fashioned way. He said, "I'm going to hit the pavement!" I was finally amenable to the idea of his living with me without marrying first. After all, we were making plans!

I began sending George job vacancies and other advertisements in his former career field and other areas of interest he had. Once again, his mother provided no positive reinforcement regarding his ideas for job searching. I finally said something because I could not watch him go through the same undermining behavior again. Surprisingly, George finally agreed with my assessment.

George told me he wanted to convince his mother to relocate to Florida too. *Oh, no!* I knew there was no way his mother would agree to come to my city. I am sure George surmised that since it was only the two of them, it could work. His siblings were smart and had built lives of their own. But it was not about the two of them, it was about George (the baby) taking a wife or significant other. History was repeating itself.

Then George stopped communicating with me completely. I was devastated. I had one big heartfelt cry. I was so heartbroken that my deceased older sister came to me in a dream and held me as I cried on her lap. When I awoke, I knew she was consoling me in my dream because she could not do it in the natural. At that moment, she was the only one who could.

CHAPTER 25

Shot Callers

In 2010, Mary retired, and Peter replaced her. Soon after, in the latter part of 2011, Peter was replaced with Jerry due to a management realignment. Along with Jerry came Tom, my new supervisor. Although I had previously met Tom, I did not know him personally.

Peter was responsible for my 2010-2011 merit evaluation, but since he did not submit it before the realignment occurred, he could no longer access my records. He gave Tom and I a copy of the narrative he had written. Tom and Jerry characterized my evaluation as "fluff" and refused to submit it. Despite Tom's and Jerry's defiance, I spoke with Peter, hoping he could somehow circumvent the system and submit the evaluation. After talking with Peter about my interaction with Tom and Jerry, he recalled a management meeting where he overheard Tom and Jerry saying that I did not deserve my position as supervisor. I failed to take heed of this omen, the harbinger for what was to come.

Tom and Jerry were setting me up for failure, and I was sure they had already selected my replacement. I wished that Peter had ensured my merit evaluation was submitted. I persistently asked for the appropriate evaluation to be utilized, but Tom refused. He wrote and submitted an impersonal evaluation, which was neither favorable nor unfavorable. I briefly considered making a formal complaint to Human Resources, but I decided against it. I wanted to avoid building an antagonistic relationship with my new managers, but I should have.

Tom and Jerry were the Shot Callers, controlling and manipulating any information about me. I recognized the underlying tactic behind not using the original "fluff" evaluation. Their tactic ensured that Tom's pending year-end evaluation of me would not garner suspicion if it was in stark contrast to the original evaluation written by Peter. By not submitting Peter's favorable evaluation, Tom could write whatever he wanted about me, and there would be no personnel record existing for comparison. Furthermore, if Peter's favorable evaluation had been submitted, it could have helped me if I had applied for a job at another agency.

After consulting with Mary regarding the evaluation tug of war, she suggested that I submit my personal yearly accomplishments along with Peter's corresponding merit evaluation. As a result, my personnel record would show Peter's favorable comments. It was a small win.

Unexpectedly, Tom extended the opportunity for me to supervise the team located in my hometown. I was shocked! I told him, *yes!* and explained that the timing was perfect because my mother was not doing well. Perhaps I should not have mentioned my mother. Instead of initiating the transfer, Tom posted the position. It was as if he had never offered it to me. I submitted a written request for a lateral transfer and Tom ignored it. I knew that others within the agency had been allowed to laterally transfer. Why should I have had to compete for a position I already had? It was then that I filed the first equal employment opportunity (EEO) claim of my entire 30-year career!

I naively believed that I could prove myself to Tom and Jerry, but I had always felt as if I was walking on eggshells. They had already made up their minds about me. Even though I was eligible for retirement in merely five years, I began applying for positions with other agencies. However, I discontinued my search after three of my male colleagues convinced me that I could do the remaining five years standing on my head. That may have been true under normal circumstances, but not with Tom and Jerry. My fate was sealed.

First, Tom wanted me to take responsibility for a poorly written investigative report submitted by team member John and approved by Supervisor Rick. I refused and reminded him that I had not approved it. Tom responded that John was now my team member. I replied that Rick was still one of Tom's supervisors and should be held accountable. Next, the agency's legal representative emailed me, requesting information about the same report. I could not believe Tom's insolence! I politely responded by email to the agency's legal representative that Rick was responsible and still supervised by Tom. Ultimately, a supervisor from an entirely different area took responsibility. Tom never addressed Rick. I questioned whether that had been another set-up. What other reason could there have been to insist on involving me?

It was finally sinking in. My presence was unappreciated. This fact became more evident after my involvement in a no-fault, minor vehicle accident. Ignoring the spirit of foreboding I felt, I used my assigned company vehicle to stop and pick up dinner at the local food court. The man who hit me was so peculiar that I could imagine his reporting me to my agency, an action that would have been much worse than if I had not reported the accident. Although there was no visible damage to my assigned company vehicle, I reluctantly phoned Tom and reported the accident. I am sure Tom was elated. Jerry and he finally had something they could use against me to further their agenda. Initially, Jerry feigned support for my situation and told me not to worry; after all, he was the top Shot Caller. Yet, I was still suspended for 30 days without pay. I knew this action was punitive, one that might not have been taken if it were anyone else in the agency with similar circumstances, but I could not prove it.

CHAPTER 26

Vincent

After George flaked out on me, I met Vincent (Vinnie), with whom I worked closely during a large, multi-agency investigation which affected several of the local post offices. Vinnie had thorough knowledge of postal operations; therefore, he made a great liaison for the case.

Vinnie was not a particularly handsome man, but he had several good qualities. First, and foremost, he was an Army veteran. Vinnie was well groomed and spoke intelligently. I enjoyed our conversations. He was also a Bible scholar. Vinnie said his father had taught him a great deal about understanding the Bible.

On our first date, we visited my most favorite place in the world, the beach! The more Vinnie spoke, the more impressive he became. I realized I was mostly attracted to his brain and the depth of his conversations. However, my attraction to his way of thinking came to a screeching halt when he too broached the subject of marriage. *Now I was beginning to believe what an inspector said to me some years ago – 'you are the marrying kind.'*

Vinnie said he was separated and in the process of a divorce. He had three children, two of them were grown. The youngest was a teenager, who seemed to be the most affected by the separation. Vinnie believed his divorce would be final in six months. He said we could marry after the divorce was final if I wanted to.

Vinnie and I may have gone out once or twice after that. I told Vinnie what happened with George and me. He said I had not gotten over George and commented that George was immature. Vinnie said I needed a man, and he was that man. I could not argue with him about George's maturity, but I was not convinced that Vinnie was the man for me.

Vinnie was dependable and behaved the way I thought a boyfriend should. When I went to Las Vegas with a girlfriend, he gave me some spending money. Vinnie became frustrated with me because I was not developing feelings for him fast enough, and he believed that was the reason for my unwillingness to be intimate with him. I, on the other hand, recognized that I still had feelings for George, and that it was just too soon for me. We continued to communicate off and on and agreed to part as friends.

Total Waste

George's disappearing act left a void in my heart. I was ready for a husband, but I still did not want to live with another man without being married. I only considered shacking up with George because it was George. I had already put so much time into our relationship and hoped that if he relocated, it would have given us the momentum the relationship needed to finally marry. However, all my efforts, thoughts and dreams were in vain.

In July 2011, while I was still recovering from my broken heart, I was on assignment in DC. It just so happened that one of the popular fraternities (of which George was also a member) had their annual conference. As I watched all the black men crowd the city and my hotel, I remembered George telling me about the conference and my telling him that I would be on assignment at the very same time. I knew he remembered. Although I did not expect George to call me, I hoped he would.

George had this non-confrontational personality. So, he hid when he was wrong instead of owning up to his actions. Hiding was even easier with the geographical distance between us. I had often observed George wait for me to call him first whenever he was being a coward. My taking the initiative to call first demonstrated to him that I was not mad or upset. It made George comfortable or confident that I was moving past the issue or problem. This character trait of George's remained constant during the latter years of our relationship. In contrast, I had observed George behave strongly and boldly with other people. Accordingly, I surmised that the cowardice was only for me. So, as I watched the men descend upon DC, I knew George was there too! Yet, I refrained from calling him. As a matter of fact, I convinced myself that I would rather break my fingers than to use them to call George.

As I entered my hotel one evening, there were several men in the lobby and one of them approached me. He was a very personable car salesman named Robert who lived in South Carolina. I allowed the conversation to begin only because I was pouting about George. Robert invited me to hang out with him and his two friends. I thought it would be fun since there was a bunch of partying going on in the city.

That night, we started the partying in this nice building with high ceilings and elaborately sculpted fountains in the lobby. I ran into a couple of female inspectors who were also enjoying the festivities. *Thank God I had packed some party clothes!* My hair was fiercely braided and styled in an up-do. So much so that I was complimented by an African male who asked me if I was from some hard to pronounce city in his country. I thought, *wow, my hair must really look authentic!*

Robert was in the city for only one night after I met him. He was nice and we exchanged phone numbers before he departed DC. After I returned home, Robert phoned me daily. He liked to call me pet names like sugar plum or sugar pop. It was a welcomed change because I was lonely. I learned he was divorced and had four adult children. After about a month, I felt our conversations had no real substance and were boring. I did not know what his motive was, but I knew he had one. I told Robert that we did not have anything in common and we stopped talking.

Another Waste

In February 2012, I prayed to God that I meet someone, but I did not give Him any precise characteristics. That was a mistake. I looked at other people around me who seemed to meet people and then have long lasting relationships. I believed my standards were unrealistic and that was why I was alone. So, after I uttered my prayer, I quickly met Tyrone.

Tyrone walked up to me while I was at the gym, sitting on the lateral pulldown machine. He was a huge, 6'4 muscular man, with arms that were huge and hard like bricks. He was not my type at all (but I had stopped having a type). He was so big that I thought men would fear him. *He could certainly protect me!* Tyrone claimed to be a colonel in the US Air Force and confidence dripped from every inch of him! When he introduced himself, he said, "My name is Tyrone. They call me Big T, but you can call me Ty."

Yet, Ty was a liar and a manipulator – the devil's spawn. He lied so much, he forgot which lie he last told – a total waste of a 6'4 man!

At first, his size alone gave the impression that he was a real man. Not only was Ty charismatic; but his confidence was intoxicating. In view of all that, something about him just did not feel right. Ty claimed to have just finished a six-year tour overseas and that he was living on the military base. Keeping that in mind, I had doubts about his being who he claimed to be. A couple of days later, while sitting at my kitchen table, I asked Ty to show me his driver's license. He told me, "That's personal!"

Ty had piqued my curiosity after responding to me in that way. I had never made such a request of anyone, but somehow this was different. I should have kicked him out of my house that very day. At the same time, I welcomed the distraction and the interaction during a time when my career was not doing well. Not only was Ty this mystery I had to solve, but he kept me preoccupied. I was determined to learn the truth about him, sooner or later.

On our first date, we went to dinner and then dancing. While riding in the car with him, Ty asked if I would consider marrying him. *Here we go again!* Since I had heard these non-committal statements about marriage before, I did not give much credence to it. I just planned to enjoy the evening. Ty continued asking that I consider marrying him after he retired from the military. When I expressed that he did not even know me, he responded, "I feel like I have known you all my life." Then he asked, "Can you be spontaneous?" I was sure that it was more suggestive than an actual question. I felt it was just a mind game to encourage, excite, and coax me to bend to his will.

After dinner, we sat in the parking lot of the night club. As I gathered my credentials to take into the club, Ty asked to see them. I looked at him and said, "I can't see yours; you can't see mine."

Then I looked over at the police car in the parking lot across from where we were parked. I was sure they were there to support the night club, standing by for any disruptions or violence. Strangely, I felt the urge to get out of the car and tell them that something was not right with the man I was with. Alternatively, I was not afraid or in distress, so I could not think of the words to describe what I was feeling to the police. I thought, *you're being paranoid, Carolyn!*

After that night, it occurred to me to use one of those people search engines. Blackbookonline.info was one that I used often for my work-related investigations. Since blackbookonline.info was not a law enforcement product, nor was it paid for through my employer, I did not risk losing my job performing the search. So, I performed a reverse look-up using Ty's cell phone number. What returned were Hispanic names of people who probably had the phone number before him, confirming that his phone number was relatively new. I surmised that Ty may have told the truth about returning from overseas after all.

After a month or so, Ty began begging for sex. It seemed that each time we talked, he brought up my not wanting to sleep with him. I wanted to continue going out with him. However, I constantly battled within regarding my decision to sleep with him or not. I thought I was strong enough to withstand his advances. But sex finally happened on the day Ty sang to me.

The night before we had sex, I could not sleep. My sleep was disturbed because of his pressuring me for sex. Ty continuously called and texted me about sex, professing how "crazy" he was about me. He said that from the moment we met, he knew I was the one for him. The unrest I experienced was the glaring, blaring sign that having sex with Ty was a bad idea.

The next morning, Ty was at my front door. He had worn me down and he knew it! Shortly after I let him in, he began singing an Isley Brother's song entitled, "For the Love of You." He could sing! Ty then swept me off my feet and carried me into my bedroom. It was like something out of a romance novel! However, the sexual act itself was not. It took him forever to have an orgasm, and I was tired of waiting.

Afterwards, I laid there with mixed feelings about Ty. He loved hearing himself talk and would not shut up! Ty said he and his ex-wife had lived in Washington, and after their divorce, he had given her $800,000. Then, he commented that we were having pillow talk and jumped up to get dressed. Ty behaved like it was out of character for him to show any kind of warmth or affection.

Within a couple of weeks, his true personality slowly revealed itself. Ty often spoke very highly of himself, as if he needed to convince me that he was all he said he was. According to him, he was still living on the military base and asked me to search for $400,000 houses for him to buy. I was a newly licensed Florida realtor and should have treated Ty as I would a client, requiring signatures for the necessary disclosures. But I knew he would not have agreed. Therefore, I was not surprised when after all my efforts, Ty told me that he had been assigned a *military* realtor. He never planned to hire me as his realtor; he purposely dangled that carrot in front of me.

Another month passed and I tried to remain excited about my relationship with Ty, despite his conversations seeming embellished. I knew that some of what he said was probably not true. I thought maybe I was being overly cautious. Afterall, Ty said he was a preacher's kid and I wanted to believe him; however, when I spoke about the Lord, I noticed that his body language showed obvious discomfort. Nevertheless, I continued to ignore my gut feelings.

Was I expecting too much from these men? I had tired of being alone and hoped Ty recognized me for the successful, independent woman that I was. *How could he not?* But the more he talked about himself, the stronger that gut feeling became that he was a liar.

Ty had swooped into my life like a force of welcomed change. My life was in utter turmoil. I had my parents' failing health on one hand and my job woes on the other. I wanted Ty to replace George and be all the things I thought George could have been. I thought Ty could take up the slack, help me make decisions, share the load, and give me a break. But it nagged me that he may not have been who he said. So, I called the military base. The person who answered the phone at the base said his name was not listed on the roster. Ty said his last name was Lawhorn. *Maybe I had the spelling wrong?* At the time, I did not realize the implications.

Ty and I continued to date for another month or so. We had gone dancing several times. Ty was an excellent dancer and we glided across the dance floor. One of our last dates was at a local casino. When the bouncer asked for identification, Ty showed the bouncer his license while noticeably shielding it from my view.

Ty bragged about being in special forces and used that as an excuse for being so secretive about everything. Once or twice, we planned a date. When he did not show up, he stated that he had an "operation." Upon speaking with one of my friends who was also a member of the national guard, she said the lingo Ty used was accurate. Nevertheless, it did not confirm he was truthful about being a member of any special investigative unit. I also had a mutual friend check his vehicle license plate. She said that no information returned and that maybe Ty was telling the truth. Still, that nagging feeling about his name not being his name, and his enormous ego, was something that I could not ignore.

Ty appeared to be well traveled. He told me he wanted us to visit a hot spring. I had no idea what that was, but I learned later there was one not far from where I lived. I was eager to experience it just because of my love for the beach. But it was an invitation that never came to fruition. He also invited me to a couples massage at one of the popular hotels. That never happened either. Whenever I followed up on these enticing invitations, there was always some alleged last-minute operation that changed his plans. Several times, a week or two would pass before I would hear from Ty. Then he would call, "Hey baby! It's Ty."

The following month, I saw Ty sparingly. He claimed he was on another mission. Ty would FaceTime me and his surroundings looked like a low-rate motel which I assumed was some military quarters. Once or twice, he phoned me alleging to be in the field. *Why would a colonel be in the field?*

Four months had passed, and I was struggling to emotionally support my mother and stepfather with their health issues, especially my mother while in the most serious fight of her life with Alzheimer's disease. I was assigned the duty of finding an assisted living facility for them both. Ty called once and said we would go out to take my mind off things, but he never followed up with that invitation either.

Honestly, once my mother's situation demanded more and more of my attention, it was very easy to distance myself from Ty. Even more so because he had shown me that he was not worthy of me. From time to time, Ty would text me, asking that I go out with him. I would text *okay* and that I was *on my way*, while lying in my bed, watching TV with no intention of meeting him. The few times that I answered his phone calls, he would try to make small talk. But when Ty heard my uninterested tone, he eventually stopped calling and texting me.

There were a couple of times that I thought Ty was following me. Once I was in the grocery store, and I looked up to see him coming towards me. When he approached me, I told him to get away from me and that he was full of that brown stuff we all defecate. Another time, I was in Sam's Club standing in the check-out line and looked up to see him watching me while sitting at the picnic style table in the snack bar area directly in front of me. That time, he did not approach me. Once I checked out, I walked in the opposite direction, away from him, and out of the store.

Ty was a habitual liar. Whenever I questioned him about something he had said, he would make up another lie to cover the first, second and third lie. I knew it was all just a game to him. I will never forget the time Ty called me and asked my whereabouts. I said, "I'm in Miami."

Then he said, "I'm stationed in Homestead now and I live in Coconut Grove."

I retorted, "You lie so much, you don't even remember the last lie you told!"

Robert

My mother's health decline took an emotional and mental toll on me. It was during this tumultuous time that I received a call from Robert. Although his call was unexpected, he seemed supportive, and I welcomed his calls.

I continued to receive daily calls from Robert. I found it strange when he began referencing a house he wanted to purchase. He gave me the address and upon researching it, I was shocked to find a beautiful, expansive, million-dollar home located just outside of Charleston, SC. I asked Robert how he would be able to afford the mortgage payments for such a home. He responded that he would be able to get a 2% interest rate loan. I did not believe that a car salesman could purchase such a home, regardless of the low interest rate. He had to be lying!

Robert made a feeble attempt at inviting himself to my home by informing me about a conference his fraternity would be holding in Tampa, FL. I had no intention of allowing him to lodge with me, however I was curious about his living arrangements in South Carolina. Therefore, I planned a road trip to visit his home. But before I could hit the road, Robert informed me of an alleged mishap.

Robert phoned me one afternoon and I noticed the stark contrast between the low voice in which he spoke and his normal elevated tone. I asked what was wrong. Robert responded that he had lost a $400 deposit received from a customer for a car. He explained that he followed the customer to a bank, located inside a Walmart, to retrieve the deposit. As he was leaving the bank and running to his car, a hard rain fell. I do not recall exactly when he discovered the money was missing, but he thought he lost it while running to his car. Robert said he retraced his steps but was unsuccessful in finding the money. Even though his explanation made no sense to me, he sounded as if he were going to cry. Robert said he considered finagling the paperwork to account for the $400 he had lost so the customer would still get credit for the down payment.

Then Robert's cell phone was disconnected. He used his office phone to call me. I thought he had probably used his own money to refund the money that he lost, and no longer had the money for his phone bill. I suggested that he use a credit card to pay his phone bill. Robert explained he did not have a credit card because his credit was affected after his divorce. He insisted that as a car salesman he needed a cell phone. After listening to his whining, I offered to loan him the money.

Considering I never told Robert that I had been suspended from work without pay and I did not have any cash, I helped him using my credit card. When I called the phone company to pay Robert's bill, he was not one but two payments behind, for a total of $375! I was sure that he purposely withheld that he owed more money, hoping that I would pay the phone bill. Once I paid the bill, Robert claimed that he also needed $100 for food until he got paid. He claimed he had given one of his children his last bit of money. In the end, Robert owed me $500. He said he would repay the money in $50 bi-weekly payments.

As soon as the first bi-weekly payment was due, Robert paid me nothing. He was still calling and talking with me, but never mentioned the money. Soon the weekend arrived for my scheduled visit with him. It was also the month of my birthday. At that time, I was still excited and expected that Robert would repay me when I arrived, but he did not.

Once I arrived, I observed that Robert's living conditions were nothing like he described. When I looked up at the ceiling fan in his bedroom, there was dust an inch thick on the blades. There was also a water flow problem in the hallway shower, and some other issue in the master bedroom bath. I could not understand why he would misrepresent himself. But since I had loaned him money, maybe he had not misrepresented himself at all.

The first evening, Robert and I went to a local chicken wing joint for dinner. When we retired for bed, I learned that although the house had 3 bedrooms, only his bedroom had a bed. One bedroom was an office and the other one contained boxes and other non-bedroom items. Although I was tempted to leave and get a hotel room, I stayed. I did not have sex with Robert, and I gave him no indication that I would – and he did not ask.

On the second day, while he worked, I toured the city. I also called a friend who lived in the area and told her what I had encountered with Robert. She invited me to stay with her. I told her thank you, but no thanks. I had made this bed and I was going to lie in it! No pun intended.

The Charleston area reminded me of Miami because of the beaches and bridges. I used one of the bridges and its surrounding path for jogging. Later that evening, Robert and I patronized two different night clubs. One was upscale and the other one was located in the 'hood.' It was very apparent that Robert did not have much money for drinks. He insisted that I drink the entire contents of my one glass of wine. When we retired for bed that night, Robert wanted to cuddle with me and pet. I told him, *stop!*

I never intended to have sex with Robert during that trip. The purpose of my trip was to check him out and determine if he were someone that I could or should have in my life. To make matters worse, Robert did not mention the money he owed me until the following morning, after breakfast.

I was sitting in my car, with my windows up and doors locked, counting the cash that I had on hand. Robert walked up to the driver's side of my car and tapped on the window. He had obviously been standing there watching me through the window counting my money. It was only then that he said, "I'm going to pay you back."

When I departed, I headed south towards Hilton Head, SC where I had already planned a two-night stay to celebrate my birthday with a massage package and some shopping! When Robert phoned me to inquire as to my whereabouts, I admitted that I was in Hilton Head. He commented that he would have met me there had I told him. I thought, *you don't have any money!*

Another two weeks passed, and Robert continued to ignore his promise to repay me. When I asked him about my money, he had another excuse. In response, I asked that he provide an update if he was not going to pay me timely. Robert seemed to take offense to my suggestion. So much so that he stopped answering my phone calls.

I did not want to believe that Robert was ignoring my calls, but he was. To confirm my suspicion, I used my co-worker's cell phone to call Robert. Sure enough, he answered. I said, "It's me. I'm calling you from a friend's phone."

His response, "Oh, my phone was broken. I just got another one."

I knew he was lying. I thought, *wow, he played me for some money.* So, I took him to small claims court for the $500 and had him served at his job! When the court date arrived, he did not show. I was told by the clerk of court that the lien would remain against him for three years. I may not have gotten my money back, but I hoped I taught him a lesson.

Instant Replay

Robert

My first impression of Robert was correct. His conversations had no substance because he was just trying to figure out how I could best serve him. Then, when I accepted his calls again, at a time when I was vulnerable and simply needed someone to talk to, he used the situation to his advantage.

Once Robert believed that I liked him, he decided to use me for money. I think he intended for me to become romantically involved with him so that I would forget about the money. But what he did not know was that although I have a big heart, I do not mix business with pleasure!

Sometimes we eat our vomit because of other things going on in our lives. Life happens and many things get in the way of our thinking logically or may even cause us to doubt our decisions. With Robert, I recognized that something was not right about him. I only doubted my decision when other things began to happen in my life, and I wanted someone to talk to. He entered my life at a time when I was heartbroken and needed someone to support me emotionally.

CHAPTER 27

Blackballers

After the suspension, my relationship with Tom and Jerry was markedly different. The atmosphere among my team was also pretentious, and I knew I had no allies. I began to pray and asked for prayer. I spoke with my mother and stepfather about my predicament. My stepfather advised that I read Psalms 35 and 91, nightly. So, for over a year, reading those chapters somehow quelled the anxiety I experienced and shielded me from the mutinous people surrounding me.

Once again, I began to apply for positions outside of my agency. I achieved the shortlist for two jobs, both in different states. I was interviewed for one position twice. During the first interview, I divulged information about the suspension for the vehicle accident. Surprisingly, I received a second interview, which gave me a glimmer of hope. However, I felt interrogated regarding the vehicle accident during the second interview, where the interviewer seemed to take pleasure in distorting the details of my account of the incident. I knew I was a good fit for the job, but she was not interested in my explanation. For the second position, I participated in a phone interview that I believed went very well. When I followed up, I sensed the interviewer had inquired with my agency about me. I knew my agency's reputation well, and nothing was confidential. I was sure I had been blackballed. Since I did not have any reliable references, I did not bother applying for any other positions.

Tom and I had several conversations regarding my team and the behaviors they displayed towards me. I remember telling him that I was not kissing my team's butts. He replied, "We don't want you to!" At one point, Tom began offering me lateral positions under his supervision. I considered receiving a saved grade and pay with no managerial responsibilities, but I refused. I had worked hard to achieve my position. Unbeknownst to me, my team's complaints fueled Tom's and Jerry's agenda.

As if that was not enough, Tom believed I had three poor performing team members – John, Susie, and Joe. I disagreed. After working with the team members for four years, I thought I was better qualified to evaluate their potential. Tom suggested that I place them on a performance improvement plan (PIP). In my experience, PIPs never accomplished what they purport – a benign strategy to get employees to focus on the mission of the agency and be more productive. The PIPs had some seemingly attainable goals within three months. The problem was it usually required more than three months to achieve the desired goals. If the employee failed to meet the goal, they would be demoted or terminated. My morals would not allow me to comply with the suggestion to issue PIPs, and I refused, choosing not to tell the agents their performance was perceived as poor.

One afternoon in 2013, Tom and Jerry came to visit my office, a fact that initially seemed harmless. However, the occurrence became strange when the clock struck 6 p.m. and I realized they had not spoken with me. One of my most productive team members alerted me that they were interviewing the others, questioning them about my management of their work and achievement of the goals and objectives. Although I appreciated the heads up, nothing could have prepared me for what happened next.

Finally, they summoned me from my office to the conference room, where Jerry began his reproach by stating that I was a good person before delving into the work ethic of team member Susie. Although Jerry was speaking, I knew he was verbalizing Tom's sentiments. Tom believed that Susie did not give a recent task the amount of attention it deserved and had previously commented on her lack of preparation, stating that she was careless. As a manager, Tom never took responsibility for problems he identified in *his* mind. Instead, he opted to blame me for the problem, and then made it appear to others that he had fixed the nonexistent problem.

I continued to listen as Jerry berated me about Susie's carelessness on a particular day. Jerry then brought into question my early departure on that same day. Tom was very much aware that I left early on that day because I called and told him that I was sick. It was clear that in relating the information about my early departure to Jerry, Tom showed his lack of empathy and omitted the fact that I had fallen ill. "I was sick!" I exclaimed, shooting Tom a stern glance. Guilt colored Tom's face as he diverted his eyes. I could not believe they were holding being sick on that one day against me, especially since I was hardly ever absent. Jerry closed with stating that team member Steve felt that I was incapable as a supervisor. I was unmoved.

What happened next? Tom and Jerry issued *me* a PIP! My assignment was to be responsible for the improvement in productivity for John, Susie, and Joe within three months. Impossible? Most definitely! But there was a caveat. If I willingly vacated my position, they would allow me to save my grade in pay and remain in my same office or relocate to my hometown, still under their supervision and control. I responded, "Let me get back with you on that."

The following day, I filed a retaliatory EEO claim, which is worse than a regular EEO. At some juncture, I recalled Tom offering me those lateral positions earlier that year and realized I could have avoided all this if I had accepted one of them. It was indeed a conspiracy.

I accepted the PIP. For the following three months, I endured a tremendous amount of stress as I complied with the PIP. Tom progressed to tormenting me via email, micromanaging me daily. I am sure a few of my team members were involved in the mutiny. My stress manifested into a strange but noticeable heaviness in my chest, and I began to gain weight.

I hired an attorney to help me with the professional ramifications of the PIP. He advised that I not take the PIP lightly. He said, "If they have given it to you, do not think that they won't use it." I also started sessions with a psychologist to ease the emotional and physical strain of the situation. While my attorney worked on my behalf with the agency's legal representative, we discussed the best alternatives for me. I could not let my job security of thirty years and retirement benefits hang in the balance of the PIP's outcome – and I am sure Tom and Jerry knew this.

Our plan was for me to leave the supervision of Tom and Jerry and choose to work in another state. But before we could draft the agreement, Tom phoned me and attempted to give me the results of my PIP – prematurely! It had only been two and a half months! I quickly contacted my attorney, who, with the help of the agency's legal representative, stopped Tom from pursuing his agenda. I knew Tom's decision would have been unfavorable for me.

It took the entire three months while on the PIP for my attorney and the agency's legal representative to write an acceptable agreement. It was by no means perfect, but it accomplished what was necessary. It was a bittersweet victory; especially when I stole Tom's thunder by being the first to notify my team of my pending departure.

During my last few days in the local office, I bid everyone farewell. I even had a luncheon at PF Changs, one of my favorite restaurants. When I visited (for the last time) the second remote office that I acquired sometime after Tom and Jerry arrived, one of the younger team members said, "It had to be someone among us who did this (to you)."

Interestingly, Steve (the one who said I was not smart enough) was also in that office. On that final day, I saw the guilt on his face and his lack of eye contact. It was confirmation that it was indeed a mutiny.

Instant Replay

My new office was one of several that was under the supervision of Peter, my former manager. It was a small field office with only two other teammates. Although Peter was not the reason that I chose the new area, it helped that I knew him. As I settled into my new office, I felt an overwhelming amount of peace. Sometimes we are not aware of what we were experiencing until we no longer are.

The resolution of my EEO claim came when I agreed to relocate and was no longer a member of Tom's and Jerry's team. However, when I learned a couple of years later that another manager had only given his team member a slap on the hand after having an *at-fault* accident in comparison to my *no-fault* accident, I filed another EEO. The agency offered me a $9,000 settlement. I refused to accept it because I needed to ensure that the agency's disparate practices were well documented by establishing a case history. In 2020, four years after my retirement, I learned that Tom was forced to leave the agency. Most believed this was due to the many EEOs filed against him. I felt vindicated!

[24] But let justice roll on like a river, righteousness like a never-failing stream! (Amos 5:24 NIV)

I *recognized* I had a problem when Tom and Jerry would not allow my merit evaluation to be submitted. I tried working it out, choosing to give the new relationship a chance, but was unsuccessful. When Peter alerted me to Tom's and Jerry's opinion regarding me and my position, I should have pushed forward with the job applications for another job and ignored the advice of my colleagues. Instead, I overlooked the feeling in my gut, the Spirit of the Lord guiding me to make a change. I only delayed the inevitable. Tom's and Jerry's punitive treatment was the vomit in which I wallowed, and it took me a long time to realize that.

Stress is a sign that you need to *purge* yourself from your surroundings or circumstances. It is often hard to leave, and it takes courage to start over. My prayers and the prayers of others helped me prepare for that fight. I finally *managed* my vomit by hiring an attorney who helped me devise a strategy to get out. I *survived* by seeking emotional counseling, venting about the drama occurring at every opportunity. I did not begin to *thrive* until I got a new beginning – on my terms. I finally understood what God wanted for me all along.

CHAPTER 28

Peace

Relocation was difficult because I did not know anyone in South Carolina. Surprisingly, I was also offered the opportunity to return to Atlanta, GA. However, I chose Columbia, SC to start anew. My attorney believed that I was well liked by my agency to be given a choice of two locations. I was certainly not well liked by Tom and Jerry, but it was not them who extended the offer.

It was apparent that Tom and Jerry offered me relocation to my hometown to shame and entice me. They thought I would accept their offer because my mother was ill. However, there was no way that I would continue working under their supervision. More importantly, my mother would not have wanted me to sacrifice my wellbeing and happiness to be closer to her. Tom and Jerry had already demonstrated their lack of appreciation for me. If I had stayed, they would have continued to harass me in some shape, form, or fashion.

I had prayed incessantly while Tom micromanaged me. After experiencing so much turmoil, I became overwhelmed and felt defeated. I turned to my friends and family for prayer weekly. One day, things got so bad that I left my desk and walked outside to phone my pastor and pray. The more prayer became a daily part of my life, the easier it was to arrive at the decision to relocate.

My mother told me many years ago, "Sometimes you have to give up something." I had traded my home in Tampa for peace and happiness. From a financial standpoint, I had lived in Tampa for five years and planned to retire there. Until that time, I had no plans to buy another home.

Once I made the decision to relocate to Columbia, SC, one of my homegirls rode with me to check it out. Our first stop was the post office where my new office would be. From there, we began to sight see, looking for places that I could shop. When I used the GPS (global positioning system) and searched for my favorite stores, we ended up in the northeast area of Columbia. I hired a realtor who was the wife of my soon to be co-worker. Using the internet, we found my new home. Things were looking good!

Surprisingly, I only rented the home for two months. Initially, I agreed to pay an additional $100 for lawn care. However, when I moved in, I noticed the grass had been poorly maintained. Feeling that I was being taken advantage of, I advised the owners that I would hire someone to cut the grass instead of paying them $100.

To make matters worse, my rent check was not received on time. I assured the owners that I had mailed it, but they did not believe me. As a result, I was forced to pay them a late fee. My landlord/tenant relationship was already off to a bad start, and I did not believe I would have any peace going forward. Since I was not happy with them and they were not happy with me, I requested to break my lease. I finally received the torn envelope with pieces of my check enclosed in a plastic bag with an apology from the post office. On the day I moved out and returned the keys to their home, I showed the owners the evidence of my payment.

After that experience, I discarded the idea of renting someone's house and decided to find an apartment. It was the first time in my life that I would rent an apartment. I chose an older development that had a three-bedroom unit with a garden tub and separate shower in the master bedroom. The rent was discounted for just under a $1000 a month for the first-year lease. That was at least a $500 a month savings in comparison to renting a house.

Before leaving Tampa, I had described to my attorney feeling a heaviness in my chest. He told me that other clients had described stress in the same way. But after being in Columbia for only a few days, I felt different. I recognized that the heaviness in my chest was gone. It was during those moments that I experienced what peace finally felt like. I knew that I had made the best decision when I chose to leave the people in Tampa and my former management behind.

Albatross

Unfortunately, I had a setback! While on surveillance for one of my cases, I was backing out of a parking space and hit a huge truck. I had checked my rearview mirrors and did not see the truck. Since the truck was parked, I was shocked that I backed into its front bumper. The nut and bolt protruding from the vanity plate scratched the left rear of my government vehicle. Although the damage to my vehicle was minor, and there was no damage to the truck, I became extremely nervous. I had a flashback and began to relive the vehicle incident that occurred in Tampa, and all the stress that came with it.

It took me three days to gather my wits and report the vehicle incident to my manager. I purposely omitted recounting the punitive treatment I received two years prior and how that caused my delay in reporting the incident. I was also afraid of how the agency would react to my having a second vehicle incident within two years. At the same time, I knew I had not done anything wrong. But because I had been harassed and mistreated, I felt like I had done something wrong. When I finally reported the vehicle incident to my manager, he expressed his disapproval of my having waited three days.

The scratch on the left rear of my vehicle was an albatross! I was in denial, but eventually I accepted that I had experienced at least two anxiety attacks during those three days. I was determined that my job performance would not be affected. So, I made an appointment with another psychologist to address my new stressor. I attended the sessions for approximately two months.

I believe that if I had scratched my government vehicle while under the management of Tom and Jerry, they would have had the option to remove me from employment. My new management perceived the vehicle incident as the minor accident it was. In contrast, Tom and Jerry would have exercised the option and used another vehicle incident as motivation to accomplish some agenda or make a statement. It confirmed that I made the best decision to depart Tampa.

CHAPTER 29

Cruise to Nowhere

After I relocated to South Carolina, Vinnie and I reconnected. He knew that the last year or so for me in Tampa was extremely difficult. So, since I had voluntarily (more like involuntarily) relocated, Vinnie called me often to check on me. He still believed he was my best choice for a future husband. Unbelievably, I had healed from the heartbreak George caused, even though we communicated every now and then. I hoped that George and I could be friends. Therefore, I considered Vinnie with an open mind and heart.

Vinnie had been promoted and was being considered for other higher-level positions within his area of work. Since I only planned to be in South Carolina for three years, after which I could retire and return to Tampa, we discussed having a long-distance relationship until I returned. Vinnie seemed to be the only man since my divorce who spoke of marriage with conviction. I could not help but think, *maybe this is the man God has for me.* So, I agreed to go with Vinnie on a 4-day, 3-night cruise to talk about our getting married.

A day or so after Christmas 2013, I flew into Tampa, FL and spent the night with my cousin. On the following day, Vinnie arrived to pick me up. When Vinnie entered my cousin's home, he walked with this confident stride. I was amazed because he acted as if he was already a member of my family. *Was he really that cocky?* I still felt some apprehension, but I was ready for a real relationship. *How else was I going to have one?*

Vinnie and I drove to Port Canaveral to embark a Carnival Cruise ship. During the drive from Tampa, we exchanged small talk. I was only a little excited about the cruise. We were cruising to the Bahamas and a private island along the return route. I was sure Vinnie expected us to seal this new direction in our relationship with sexual intimacy. However, my body did not cooperate with the plan.

In the first six months of that year, I had experienced a menstrual cycle every three months, a definite sign of menopause. But in the latter six months of the year, I had not experienced a period at all. I was sure that was the last I had seen of my unwelcomed thirty-seven-year visitor. Strangely, my period visited me for the very last time during the cruise. It was incredible! Although Vinnie did not complain, I am sure he did not believe me. I imagined he checked the waste baskets for used and disposed sanitary items.

The first few days of the cruise were pleasant and uneventful. At the dinner table, we had been assigned seating with a pastor and his wife, a pair of newlyweds, and an older military couple. We were the only unmarried couple. The conversations had been lighthearted and entertaining. Vinnie seemed to gravitate towards the military couple, specifically the husband. He and Vinnie appeared to have much in common.

The last evening was formal night and we dressed very nicely. I wore a semi-formal, fitted black velvet dress with spaghetti straps. Vinnie wore a dark colored suit. It was on that night during dinner that my groove was interrupted. The conversation began lightheartedly as it had on the previous evenings. Suddenly, the mood changed, and the focus was on our relationship and whether we planned to marry. Vinnie explained that the purpose of our cruise was to discuss marriage. Then the two remaining couples, absent the military retiree and his wife, began offering marital advice. Each couple had several thought-provoking comments. I do not remember exactly what they said, but one comment related to marriage being a contract. Their delivery was everything but romantic and the impact on me was intense. I do not believe in coincidences, but when those couples finished talking with us, I knew that Vinnie was not the man for me.

Vinnie was angry when we returned to our cabin. He said, "They can't tell me about marriage...I know what it means to be married!"

Vinnie continued, exclaiming that he did not need any advice. I, on the other hand, felt my disposition had changed. It was as if something came over me and I had not felt that way at the beginning of the cruise. I was extremely uncomfortable, and I told Vinnie something was not right. To make matters worse, I told him that if I had not had my fickle period, we still would not have been sexually intimate.

"What?!" Vinnie's tone was extremely annoyed.

At that time, I could not explain (nor did I know) that I felt the presence of the Spirit of the Lord counseling me.

[3] 'Call to me and I will answer you and tell you great and unsearchable things you do not know.' (Jeremiah 33:3 NIV)

On the next morning, while packing, Vinnie commented, "I could have stayed home for this!"

As I looked over at him, I knew he believed his time and money had been wasted. I could not blame Vinnie for feeling that way. Our romantic adventure had not culminated as he or I expected.

Then Vinnie began looking frantically for his cell phone. I watched him search for it in his luggage. Vinnie had two bags and he concentrated his search on the smaller bag that looked like a soft leather briefcase. I assisted by searching in other areas of the room. Once he tired of looking, he reported the cell phone missing to the lost and found area of the ship.

As we sat awaiting disembarkation, I apologized to Vinnie for our failed attempt at discussing a marriage between us. I tried to explain my change of heart and the feeling of unrest. But I could not.

When we finally arrived at Port Canaveral, Vinnie took me to the Orlando Sanford International Airport. It seemed a very short drive from the cruise terminal. Before Vinnie and I separated, he retrieved a backup cell phone from the trunk of his car – really. He asked me to save the phone number in my contacts. Imagine my surprise when two days later, I received a phone call from the missing cell phone. Only it was not Vinnie but a mysterious woman professing to be his girlfriend of five years.

The woman wanted to know what my relationship was with Vinnie. I assured her that Vinnie and I were just friends and that I did not know anything about her. Since nothing had happened between us while on the cruise, I did not tell a lie.

Instant Replay

Vinnie's wife had passed away a year or so prior to our cruise trip, and sometime after their divorce. I knew Vinnie's ex-wife had been sick for a while. I also recalled his talking about a relationship with a woman that was long over. The woman seemed very annoyed that I knew about Vinnie's ex-wife and not about her. But it appeared that their relationship began and ran concurrently while Vinnie was married.

I was willing to settle for the vomit of desperation. Vinnie was the one who seriously talked about marriage. He constantly reassured me of his financial stability, eventually collecting two pensions – one from the US Army and a second one from his then current job. Considering all that, the Spirit within me would not let me settle.

The Spirit of the Lord protected me from getting involved with Vinnie. The signs were there – the forewarning from the couples and that cloud of doubt and hesitation that engulfed me. I felt it so strongly that I could not ignore His message. I wanted to be in a marriage, and I almost sacrificed myself for that cause. You must pay attention. The signs may not be as vivid as they were for me during that experience, but there is always a sign.

CHAPTER 30

The Call

In January 2014, my life took a sharp turn. Do you remember Cookie? She was my ride or die, the one friend who always had my back. Well Cookie needed my support while experiencing the effects of an ugly divorce. She sought prayer from my mother and expressed to me that she wished my mother could pray for and with her. But my mother, once a strong prayer warrior, was unable to pray for or with anyone.

I did not know it then, but I had to pay it forward simply because of the prayers that were said for me. When my team, and Tom and Jerry were causing me stress, those prayers kept me sane and afloat. I volunteered to pray for Cookie on behalf of my mother.

Whenever Cookie called me to vent, I sent her a daily prayer via text message in response. During the succeeding two months, two additional friends, one each month, confided in me that they were experiencing deep depression and even suicidal thoughts because of relationship woes. I then realized that a calling had been placed on my life and it was my turn to become a prayer warrior.

My sharing daily text message prayers with three women, evolved into my sharing daily email prayers with many. I had not fully grasped the meaning of what had begun, but I knew the prayers were helping others based upon the feedback I received from my readers. I named the daily prayers, *Prayer Share*. Soon, I would learn exactly what the *Prayer Share* meant for my life.

By July 2014, my commitment to *Prayer Share* led my spiritual transformation and my physical desires collided with the new direction my life had taken. I immediately began praying to God. *Why can't I be more like others?* Briefly, I longed for the complacency I had witnessed in countless people, but I heard the Spirit say, "You are different." At that moment, I knew I needed to change some things in my life. But there was not an instant transformation.

Tyrone

In October 2014, a little over a year after moving to South Carolina, I used a ruse to contact Ty. I saw it as an opportunity to finally solve the mystery of who he was and what he was hiding. He just so happened to be in Augusta, GA, only an hour and a half away from.where I lived. I was not surprised he was in Augusta because the only thing I believed about him was that he was in the military. Of course, Ty used the opportunity to ask for another chance with me. *Another chance to lie to me some more? I don't think so!* But I knew that if I allowed him to spin more lies, he would become comfortable and slip up – and he did.

On a mission to learn the truth, I met Ty in Augusta. After refusing to park my car and ride with him, I followed him to an informal seafood restaurant. He was still driving the same vehicle with a Florida tag, so I memorized his license tag number just in case it became important. After dinner, we went dancing in some hole in the wall club near the military base. While at the bar, Ty invited me to Las Vegas for the weekend. I was sure he was lying again.

Afterwards, we went to a house that he claimed belonged to a friend of his. No one was at home. We entered the home through the garage. I could only see the kitchen and another room, where I got a glimpse of a few family pictures before ascending stairs to the bonus room. The bathroom, located in the bonus room, was filthy! The toilet seat had a brown crusty film on it which looked like a combination of dead skin, oil and sweat. It was disgusting! Fortunately, there were cleaning products under the sink which I used generously.

That night, Ty apparently got my unspoken message that there would be no sex between us. He did not beg, nor did he make advances toward me. During the very few hours of sleep I got, I dreamed about spiders. I knew that spiders were not a good omen. When I mentioned the dream to Ty the next morning, he said spiders were good luck. *That man would say anything to spin a situation to his advantage!*

Ty was in Augusta for about two to three more weeks. When he visited me in Columbia, he continued with his game about our getting married after he retired. By then, his alleged retirement date was only a few months away. We even went to Jared! While at Jared, Ty encouraged me to try on a five-carat diamond ring and pretended that it was something he wanted to buy for me. Then he casually asked me if *I* had an account there! I thought, *you have really lost your mind!*

Ty finally made a mistake. When he sent me one of his many, *I need attention* text messages, instead of his phone number identifying him as the sender, it was an email address. *Good ole iPhone!* The email address showed 'tyroneshaw@hotmail.com.' Two years prior, Ty said his name was Tyrone Lawhorn. But this time, he corrected me when I pronounced it *Lawhorn* and said, *its Longhorn not Lawhorn.*

Ty was emphatic regarding his last name being Longhorn and proceeded to show me a picture on his phone of a musician whose last name was also Longhorn. He said, "Don't I look like him?" Ty tried to convince me that the man was his grandfather. The picture appeared to be the result of an internet search. With that revelation, I later used the Google search on my phone and was able to find the exact same picture. Because of the alleged mispronunciation of his last name, I was even more convinced that he lied about his last name. However, after receiving the text message with an email address for the sender, it confirmed that his last name was not Longhorn or nowhere near it.

About two months passed and I heard from Ty again. I knew he would eventually call because he thought it was always about him. It was during December 2014, I received two FaceTime calls within 5 minutes. I ignored the calls.

A couple of months later, Ty called me again. I was driving while traveling for one of many work assignments. He claimed he had retired and hoped we could get together. I told him I was dating someone. Ty mumbled as if talking to someone else, "She couldn't even wait for me to get out of the military."

Ty behaved like his limited presence in my life, which included disappearing for weeks and calling me whenever he was bored, constituted a relationship. Ty's response was ego driven. He believed I should have waited for him because he thought he was all that.

Then, one evening Ty called and said he was in Columbia again. He invited me to meet him at a night club that I was familiar with. Since I was bored, I got dressed and went to the night club. When I called Ty to see if he was there yet, he said, "You running late?"

I said, "No, I'm here."

I could tell by his voice that he was taken aback. I waited a few minutes, and then he said, "Go on in!"

When I went inside the club, I walked around for a moment until I realized that Ty had stood me up again! He was not in Columbia. It confirmed that Ty was never in any of the places he claimed to be. It was just part of the hide and seek game Ty liked to play.

During another long pause from the last time I heard from Ty, I decided to perform another reverse look-up on blackbookonline.info. Using Ty's phone number, the search disclosed everything I expected. The report only cost me about two bucks! Ty's name was Michael T. Shaw. His address showed that he lived in a subdivision that would have been five minutes from where I had previously lived in Florida. Washington was one of the three states shown with previous residences.

I remember seeing the name of the adult child he had mentioned to me once or twice. I did not see a female listed with his last name, but I felt sure that he was probably married. In comparison to what he had said about himself, several things matched. Rather, he was in the US Army, not the Air Force.

The next time Ty called me, I confronted him. "I know your last name is Shaw."

I showed no emotion because by that time I could not have cared less. Accordingly, I planned to never speak with him again.

Ty responded, "That's what they call me."

Then I said, "You even lied to me about your name."

He said, "I can't have a hyphenated last name?"

I disconnected the call. *He is still trying to cover another one of his lies.* That was the last time Ty called me or I called him.

Spiritual Transformation

My brother Charles was an educator and a retired high school principal. He was extremely dedicated to educating his students. He continued mentoring students well after his retirement. It was concerning for Charles that I had been divorced twice and had yet to find a mate. I believe he thought marriage would complete me. While attending his funeral, I learned through one of his colleagues that he had asked, "Do you have anyone for my sister to meet?" It warmed my heart.

In December 2014, when I was reintroduced to Wesley (Wes), it seemed that Charles had gotten his wish. Wes was a friend of my favorite cousin, someone I remembered from back in the old days. Since I had introduced my cousin to his wife, he was returning the favor. Wes was a tall slender, 6'1 man. He was popular in his circle. Therefore, he was overly concerned about how he was perceived by others.

Wes was also an educator, someone whom my brother would have approved. He was intelligent so we had great conversations. It was a good relationship in the beginning. Wes was attentive and called me daily. He only lived a couple hours' drive away from me, so the long distance was not an issue. He wanted the relationship and I thought I wanted it too. By May 2015, I became uncomfortable with the direction in which the relationship was going.

I had been writing the daily devotionals for over a year and had not been involved in any serious relationships. I was finally in a relationship that had the potential to become serious. At the same time, I felt the Spirit of the Lord admonished me for spreading God's Word with an unclean spirit.

Wes was very much aware of the *Prayer Share* and received my daily email. He appeared to be supportive and often replied to my devotional emails with encouraging feedback. Wes was also involved in his church and awfully close to his pastor. Consequently, I felt that if anyone would understand my feelings and desire to change the level of intimacy in our relationship, it should have been Wes. Not to mention that I had evolved to a point in my life where I wanted sex to mean something more than a physical, perfunctory act. I wanted to be in love with, and married to, my sexual partner.

I began my conversation with Wes by laying out all my concerns. Wes responded, "No one has ever been concerned about my salvation before."

That was deep. Consequently, I asked Wes if he thought I was someone he could consider marrying. "Absolutely," was his response.

By no means was I pressuring him. I simply explained that I no longer wanted sexual intimacy in a relationship without marriage. I felt somewhat guilty about misleading him and wished I had recognized beforehand how the *Prayer Share* would transform me. The Spirit of the Lord had subtly encouraged me along my path.

The following month, I was Wes' guest at an event. The encounter was awkward because I attempted to behave as though nothing had changed, but Wes exhibited discomfort and his warmth had disintegrated. Wes admitted that it was difficult for him to continue seeing me due to my stance on abstinence and asked if I missed sex. I lied and said *yes*, but I had not missed sex. I especially did not miss sex with Wes because I was not in love with him. Abstinence forced me to realize that Wes could not provide me with what I wanted. I longed for love, and I was not in love with Wes.

Wes and I continued to communicate daily for another few months. But he showed me my place in his life when he planned a road trip in September 2015 and did not mention it to me. I learned of the trip on the morning of his departure. I believed he did not want me to even consider accompanying him because he had another woman with him.

Ironically, that same morning I was also taking a road trip to Atlanta. Therefore, I was not too bothered about his deception. Wes said he would call me once he was on the road. It was not until after 5 p.m. that day that I realized Wes had not called me. Some time that evening, I received a text message from Wes claiming to have experienced poor cell phone reception the entire drive. Then Wes sent me a picture of a "Welcome to New York" billboard to corroborate arriving at his destination.

The following day, I did not receive my daily phone call from Wes. Yet I received an email from him claiming to be experiencing continuous cell phone issues. I remembered he was scheduled to report for work within the next day or two, so I decided that I would speak with him then. When two days had passed and I still had not spoken with Wes, I called his job. The receptionist stated that he would be out of the office for the entire week. Immediately, I knew something was wrong. Wes did not take extra days off. Consequently, I believed the days off were unscheduled and something had indeed happened.

Five days became seven days, and then 14 days lapsed without a call from Wes. As each day passed, I became more and more worried about him. My daily *Prayer Share* devotionals were centered around the concern I had for Wes. I asked God for peace as

I waited for Wes to contact me. Even though I did not like that Wes concealed his road trip from me, it was not like him to do a total disappearing act. Finally, after being missing in action for 14 days, I received a call from Wes on day 15, around 8 p.m. on a Monday evening.

I said, "Hello?"

Wes said, "Carolyn, you are not going to believe this, but I have been in the hospital for 14 days! ... I was praying for you because I knew you were worried about me."

Wes claimed to have gotten a bad case of food poisoning at some restaurant located in Manhattan. He explained that he had just gotten a new phone and that contributed to his delay in contacting me. Wes said he had not memorized my phone number, and therefore he could not have called me sooner. I wondered if his companion got food poisoning too. I was 98% sure he had a companion when he started his trip. Wes did not speak with me long. By the time he called me back, he was almost home. *Didn't he have to pass my exit on the interstate on his way home?*

Wes resumed his daily phone calls through the month of October. I could not help but think that if he had not been secretive and dishonest about his trip, he would not have gotten food poisoning. *That's how God works!*

Around the end of October 2015, I received a long text message from Wes discontinuing our relationship. He explained, in short, that he had some family issues that required his undivided attention. I simply said, *okay*. After that, I received a text message on Thanksgiving Day and a final text message on Christmas Day.

Reconciliation

I finally saw George again after five years had passed and I had retired. It was in December 2016. In the years prior, I communicated with George every so often. I knew he had started his own business and I was happy for him.

I had hoped to feel the love or excitement that I had experienced with George with someone, but it had not happened. During our first dinner date, I explained to George about my daily devotionals and my pending Christian book, *Prayers of My Mother*. He asked, "What made you want to write a book?"

I responded, "I was compelled to write it!"

So, when we had dinner for a second time during my stay in his city, I was taken aback when George asked for a reconciliation. He added that his mother was encouraging him to settle down. George apologized for what had transpired between us five years prior. He said he was non-committal because he did not want to come to me with his tail between his legs. George asked for an additional year because he wanted to be in a certain financial position with his business. It was easy for me to say, *yes*. But I had a condition. I told George, "I cannot sleep with you!"

It took George several months to understand exactly what that would mean for us. However, because of my nine-year experience with George, I would have had the same stipulations even if my path had not changed.

I believed that simply abstaining from sex would *manage* the vomit of disappointment that I had once experienced with George. But it was not enough. George still disappointed me because when the year was over, he was not ready.

For another three years, I was his friend. George spoke several times about visiting me during those four years, but he never did. Each time he said he would visit, I secretly panicked because I did not think I was strong enough to withstand the temptation that George represented for me. But all my worry was in vain because none of the plans he spoke materialized and the excuses were always about his work, work that he could have controlled because he had his own business.

It appeared that George had finally attained the six-figure salary that he sought, and a personal relationship with me was never a priority, again. George even used his work as an excuse when my mother passed away in December 2020. Sadly, I was not surprised. When my mother's health took a turn for the worse, I knew her death would reveal if George could really be available for me. I hoped that above all else, George and I were friends. But when he was not emotionally available for me, I was forced to accept that we were not friends, and he would not change.

[9] What has been will be again, what has been done will be done again; there is nothing new under the sun. (Ecclesiastes 1:9 NIV)

Instant Replay

Tyrone

Ty possessed many characteristics of a sociopath. He was egocentric and lacked empathy. The sequence of events confirmed that I was eating the vomit of deceit, packaged by Satan himself. Ty presented himself at the most opportune time, right after my prayers were uttered for a mate. But I was not specific in my prayer. Yes, somehow the devil knows what you want to hear and that is how you are deceived in the first place.

Ty rushed into my life during a tumultuous time. He was in a hurry because he only had a limited amount of time to manipulate as many women as he could before he established a permanent residence. Not only was I lonely and recovering from heartbreak, but my vulnerability was more pronounced because of my mother's health challenges with Alzheimer's, and my career struggles.

I was wooed before I believed Ty was a liar. My gut was telling me one thing, but my heart wanted something else. I believed he was who he purported to be – I was so easily misled. If I had not slept with him, it would not have been important to know who or what he was. Ty may not have physically raped me, but he raped my spirit. I freely gave myself to him because of whom I thought he was and not who he really was, and he gladly accepted without remorse. That was how Ty manipulated women, and I fell for it.

Ty was either a trained liar or an accomplished one. His lying was believable because of his presentation. It was my gut – the spirit within me, that screamed almost the entire time that he was a fake. I wanted the fantasy. Even when I realized he was lying, I did not think I would succumb to it.

Special operations or not, I was convinced that Ty was in the military, just by his stature and physique. He even claimed to speak another language besides English, which I am sure was another lie. Either way, Ty was a convenient distraction to keep my mind off the chaos occurring around me. I could have been in danger allowing him in my atmosphere and life. There were times that I forgot Ty was a liar – he was just that good at it! Even in the end, I wanted Ty to admit his deception. But he continued to lie even when I confronted him with his truth.

When you are involved with deceitful and manipulative people, you will be affected. It is hard to be strong and keep your feelings separate. Therefore, you should stay away from people who are liars. When they lie to you once, they will lie again. In the words of the late, great, Aretha Franklin, you will forget "who's zoomin' who?"

I never forgot the dream I had about spiders. I used the dreammoods.com website to find the meaning of my dream. It indicated the following about spiders:

> *To see a spider in your dream indicates that you are feeling like an outsider in some situation. Or perhaps you want to keep your distance and stay away from an alluring and tempting situation. The spider is also symbolic of feminine power or an overbearing mother figure in your life. Alternatively, a spider refers to a powerful force protecting you against your self-destructive behavior.*

This dream was a sign for what was happening to me at that precise moment in my life. I wanted to stay away from Ty, but at the same time, I was determined to solve the mystery. I was never afraid of him, but I should have been. It was extremely important to me that I end Ty's charade and ensure he knew that I knew the truth. In essence, it should not have been that important. Once I believed in my gut that he was a liar, I should have stopped answering his calls.

Spiritual Transformation

My close friends believed that I was in a good relationship with Wes. Initially, I was happy. Perhaps if I were not writing the daily devotionals, I would have nonchalantly continued the relationship with Wes. Maybe it would have eventually led to marriage, maybe not.

There are many Christians straddling the fence. They have sex outside of marriage and justify their actions with alleged committed relationships. Many of those relationships do end in marriage. I am not judging, only God can judge. As for me, my spirit was not at peace when I straddled the fence.

Reconciliation

George and I had that final break in May 2011. Our limited plans never came to fruition. Our relationship had struggled for nine years. I knew George loved me, but he desperately wanted support from his mother, support that never came. It did not make things any easier when George's father left them.

Then another five years later, in December 2016, when George asked me for a reconciliation, I really thought George was ready. And when George said that his mother was encouraging him to settle down, I was sure the Lord had answered my prayers.

I never told anyone about my prayers for George. In 2011, I had asked the Lord to release the hold that George's mother had on him so that he could come into his manhood. I believed his mother made him feel guilty about wanting a life of his own. I was also convinced that his father had put unreasonable expectations on George to be the man for his mother that his father had not been. My prayers for George were never about me, perhaps they should have been.

Part VI – The Final Score

[11] As a dog returns to its vomit, so fools repeat their folly. (Proverbs 26:11 NIV)

The key to overcoming the vomit in our lives is *recognizing* or identifying unhealthy relationships and patterns of destructive behaviors. Vomit, most times is not a specific person, but our repeated behavior with certain people or their repeated behavior with us. It also emerges during situations in which we are so intertwined with certain people that we attempt to *manage* the relationships, situations and/or the people. Too many times we are unsuccessful. It is when we are unsuccessful that we must *purge* those situations or people from our lives to *survive* and *thrive*.

CHAPTER 31

Career Vomit

Today, it is easier to prepare for a successful career by simply utilizing the internet to research a desired career field. Whether you are college bound, technically savvy, or an entrepreneur, the internet will reveal information you need to plan. The internet may also reveal people who are doing what you want to do. Reading their backgrounds and experiences may help perfect a career path or model. Whatever your career goals, you must plan accordingly.

It was Benjamin Franklin who said, "If you fail to plan, you plan to fail." There will be things you cannot plan for. Situations will arise and it will not be the textbook scenario or what the research disclosed. Yet, if you have planned and the unexpected happens, your research may have prepared you for that too!

Many times, I was not prepared for adversity. I was confident and determined to achieve my objectives, so I persevered. As a victim of abuse, I was stronger and even fearless because of my experiences and circumstances. It was that strength that made me a desirable law enforcement candidate and I embraced the opportunity. Besides, what more could anyone do to me that I could not overcome?

As I recap my career challenges and triumphs, there were certain behaviors or signs that indicated I was experiencing career vomit. Let's review them.

Recognizing your Vomit

You must **recognize** when you are perceived as a threat. I was shocked to learn that two supervisors and one manager deliberately thwarted three job opportunities early in my career. They obviously recognized my potential to be successful, perhaps even more successful than them. Therefore, they took advantage of their role in my career and stopped me before I could begin. I was young and believed that an excellent work ethic warranted a fair evaluation. I learned that corporate culture dictated that fair evaluations resulted from more than just hard work. Know your organization's culture!

Amid my law enforcement accomplishments were always the small but significant setbacks. Most significant was not getting my very first case prosecuted. If it had been prosecuted, I would have been considered for detail and promotional opportunities earlier in my career and my resume would have reflected that prosecution and the others that would have followed.

Much later in my career, I encountered managers who had unwarranted negative preconceptions of me. The managers manipulated organizational policy to demonstrate their power and bully me. But God had the power!

You must **recognize** when you are defeated. Acknowledging defeat in one area, does not mean you cannot find victory in another. Initially, I did not understand the organization's culture. My objective was to become known, impress managers, and consequently be offered a detail. But my efforts were in vain. The who-you-know politics were quite blatant. Not to mention the managers who "spear-headed" individuals for certain positions. However, I was ready when that vacancy surfaced – the one without a pre-selected candidate. Have your resume ready!

Once warned that my new management believed I was not deserving of my position, I should have taken heed and planned my next move. I pivoted several times in my career, before recognizing when it was time to move on. However, that one time (with Tom and Jerry), I stayed too long and was too slow to react. It was a hard-earned lesson. Have an exit strategy!

You must **recognize** when you have discernment. Discernment is that gut instinct that you only realize after ignoring it hundreds of times. I have it. You have it. When you get that gut instinct, you doubt what you are thinking or feeling. It is only after you regret ignoring what you thought or felt, that you begin to believe in your gut instinct. Many times, that instinct is discernment – the Spirit of the Lord speaking to you. Trust your instincts!

Ignoring discernment to find another job after I sensed a planned sabotage, was a mistake. Had I followed through, and not allowed colleagues to persuade me, I am sure I would have landed a better job, with better managers. Later, when I ignored discernment a second time, which felt more like a foreboding, I missed another opportunity to prevent an event that ultimately decided my fate. If only I respected discernment – the Spirit of the Lord attempting to get my attention. Perhaps, my fate was already sealed. Take heed!

You must **recognize** a mutiny. A mutiny is harder to discern because the target – you, are the last to know. In my case my team converged and plotted my demise. The first sign was the ridiculous complaints alleging things I did or did not do. Do not be complacent!

Know your company's policies. If management goes above and beyond to treat you punitively in comparison to others, and tells you their hands are tied because of policy, you are not appreciated or respected. Find another job!

Managing your Vomit

You must **manage** your circumstances. When you are so deeply immersed in a situation, you will lose the ability to see things objectively. You become complacent and believe your circumstances should continue as they are, even when you know deep down you need to make a change. Rarely will you be successful if you do not make a change. Sometimes, God manages your circumstances for you.

I managed my applications for promotion by circumventing the supervisors and managers who wanted to sabotage my efforts and prevent me from attaining a promotion. God managed my circumstances when He introduced supervisors and managers into my life who supported my promotional efforts and even shielded me on two occasions from losing my job. Know your supporters!

Purging your Vomit

You must **purge** the *things* that have you bound. It is difficult to purge or remove yourself from a job, especially if it is your main source of income. When co-workers, whether subordinates or management, interfere with your quality of work, health, or both, you must consider obtaining another job. Plan your next move!

Office politics are difficult to combat. If you are aware of office politics beforehand, it just may provide a competitive advantage. Often, you learn that office politics exist when it is too late. I continuously worked to improve my relationships with my subordinates and management; nothing helped. Their concerted efforts to resist me and my authority took a toll on my health. The corporate culture, also known as politics, supported their behavior and I had nowhere to turn for help within the organization. Beware of office politics!

Surviving your Vomit

You can **survive** because of the guiding stars (angels), mentors, and allies you have along the way. It helps to have someone in your corner to lead and guide you throughout your career. Sometimes God intercedes and places people in just the right place to help you. Recognize your stars!

I faced adversity in the workplace my entire career. God consistently placed stars and mentors who helped guide me along my path to accomplish whatever His plans were for me. You must take the initiative to get what you need when you need it. There are many guiding stars, mentors, and allies available in the workplace. Do not be afraid to seek or ask for help!

Thriving After your Vomit

Thrive with union or attorney representation, and continuous prayer. I could not have imagined that during the last three years of my 33-year career, I would have been in the biggest fight to keep my job! I could have retired at the 25-year or 30-year milestone. If I had, I would have forfeited 18% of my pension – and that was not an option. I am positive their plan was to force me to retire prematurely. Sometimes, the answer to your prayers may involve seeking union representation or hiring an attorney – to assist you with thorough planning so that you refrain from reacting hastily. Either way, document when you are the victim of disparate treatment. Justice will prevail!

CHAPTER 32

Relationship Vomit

The major difference between relationship and career vomit, is that relationships mostly involve specific people. We are so attached to certain people that we believe we cannot live without them in our lives. It is not just the sexual relationship that ties us to these people, but also our emotions. Emotional attachments are stronger because they connect our entire being – physical, psychological, and spiritual.

When those people do not feel the same about us, it becomes a problem. We do more to have them in our lives and do not realize they are doing less. We are doing what makes us happy and they love being on the receiving end of our attention. Eventually, they will move on, and we will feel the loss. They will not feel anything because they did not feel the same about us. They were just enjoying the attention. This is when we must change our behavior with certain people. Henry Ford, the founder of Ford Motor company, put it best,

"If you always do what you always did, you will always get what you always got!"

As I recap my relationships, there were certain people that my repeated behavior with them or their repeated behavior with me indicated I was experiencing relationship vomit. Let's review some key indicators.

Recognizing your Vomit

You must **recognize** when you have been or are being abused. It is not stupidity. Abuse usually begins subtly and gradually grows stronger. There are at least three types of abuse – physical, verbal, and psychological/emotional abuse. The abuser gains your trust and love, and then his or her behavior changes. The changes are accepted at first because they are minor things. You do not believe the aggressor means any harm or that his/her behavior is intentional because you love them and believe they love you.

Eventually, you measure the good behavior versus the bad behavior, and that determines how long you will tolerate them. He/She is good *most* of the time. Know the signs!

In my experience, insecurity, jealousy, and intimidation influenced abusive behavior. The need to dominate, control, and feel superior were constant themes. Underlying reasons were family background or upbringing, educational or professional status, and financial stability in comparison to mine. I am sure there are other triggers for abusive relationships. The abusers do not care what kind of person you are on the inside, or what you look like on the outside.

In my second marriage, my spouse was intimidated by my career status. His underlying goal was to negatively affect my career. He knew that if I was in a domestic dispute, I could lose my job. Therefore, he attempted to goad me into physical altercations. Losing my job would have decreased me to a level that made him more comfortable. I would have been inferior, and he would have felt superior. Know the triggers and consequences!

You must **recognize** when you are settling. Even when you know your current relationship is not working, you settle. You fear starting over because you are desperate to have someone in your life. Once you start anew, you regret the time you wasted, especially when you knew better in the first place. Do not be afraid. Have no regrets!

My heart has been broken twice. Each time I wanted to reconcile those two relationships, simply because I knew the men – like I knew the back of my hand. I understood them. But could I really trust them again? I wanted what was familiar versus starting over. I held on to whatever little attention I received in each relationship and settled for whatever excuses I was given. I convinced myself the attention was enough, and the excuses were reasonable. Finally, I accepted the excuses were not reasonable. Do not settle!

You must **recognize** when you have discernment. When you are in a relationship, your heart, thoughts, and feelings cry out when your gut instincts are disturbed. I had discernment several times in each of my relationships. I did not take heed at first. It was only after ignoring my thoughts and feelings several times that I finally understood which thoughts and feelings were from the Spirit. Trust your instincts!

You must **recognize** when you have been or are being manipulated. When my mother had the "talk" with me about sexual intercourse, what I remember most is my mother saying, "You can't stop once you start." The magnitude of sex in our lives is not emphasized enough regarding the manipulation that people use to achieve the sexual encounter. When sex is easily attainable, it is not a challenge, and people do not resort to manipulation. However, some people prefer a challenge. It is even more satisfying to some people when they lie, cheat, or misrepresent themselves to have a sexual relationship. A skilled lover is the worst manipulator. Not to mention the people who will use manipulative tactics just to keep others from having a sexual relationship with you or you from having a sexual relationship with someone else. Stop the madness!

My mother had three sons. She purposely did not interfere when her sons chose their mates. There is a saying, "Mothers raise their daughters (to be independent) and love their sons. I googled the latter to learn its origin. Several articles and quotes returned. But the most applicable was an article written by Madame Noire contributor and columnist Lashaun Williams. In short, Williams states, "We connect with our daughters and, in a sense, often push them to heights we have never reached." I can relate to this statement wholeheartedly because as a single parent, I raised my daughter to be independent. Williams continues, "...Too many mothers coddle their sons through life—loving them as boys but not raising them to be men...it is that mama's boy inclination that fosters irresponsibility, unaccountability and laziness." In other words, mothers should raise their sons to be independent too!

Sadly, there are parents who manipulate their adult children just because they do not want their adult children to be involved in a specific relationship. Conversely, there are adult children who allow their parents to be manipulative and interfere in their relationships because they are not ready to give a specific relationship the level of commitment required. In some cases, it would be best if parents did not interfere with their adult children's relationships.

It becomes harder for those who are constantly manipulated to discern whether someone is being open and honest or just manipulative. Constant manipulation interferes with their ability to love objectively. If you are the manipulator, what kind of person are you? Do not be selfish!

You must **recognize** when you are being deceived. Have you ever wondered why some people have chosen to lie instead of telling the truth? I have resolved that it is their perception of you and themselves. Not far behind are the motives behind their lies. How hard can it be to tell the truth? We need a Truth Revolution!

People sometimes sell an image, instead of just being themselves. They lack confidence and think a little "white" lie will not matter. At other times, people are hiding something. Is there a difference between knowing and loving someone intimately, who is living a double life; and knowing and loving someone who is pretending to be someone else. This person could be one in the same. Bottom line, the people who will get hurt are those who believed in the deceiver.

When someone lied to me about his identity, my instincts alerted that he was hiding something. I thought I was overreacting, and I downplayed my suspicions. Instead, I should have demanded identification, called the police, or kicked him out of my life. Later, when I learned my suspicions had merit, I was ashamed that I doubted myself and got sucked into his game. That situation could have ended very badly. Follow your instincts!

You must **recognize** the backstabbers. It hurts when someone you consider your best friend, or even a family member stabs you in the back and twists the knife. It usually happens because of jealousy, plain and simple. Someone wants the attention or something else you have. Backstabbers cannot have your life. They must be satisfied with their own. Stop the haters!

You must **recognize** innuendos. Some men/women will make crass or sexist remarks. Such remarks are by no means flattering. Perhaps such comments were fruitful in some past situation or circumstance. However, if no one objects, the crass/sexist remarks will continue. Demand respect!

You must **recognize** that you will be disappointed. If you allow it, the heartbreaking, gut wrenching situations will happen repeatedly until you learn that he or she will always disappoint you. Remember, "If you always do what you always did" with certain people, "you will always get what you always got!" Make the change!

You must **recognize** that love is blind. Love is a "many-splintered" thing. Surviving love's impact is never simple. As women, particularly, and men, we are not taught early in life to profile our potential mates. Therefore, we learn by trial, tribulations, and error. You need criteria!

As I recapped the ghosts of relationships past, I am haunted by what I do not want in a relationship. What should you want? The basics – love, respect, and honor. We learn love from our parents and other members of our family. But if we have not experienced it, we cannot emulate it in our own relationships. The same follows for respect and honor.

The heart wants what the heart wants. You give a lot of time and energy into relationships, sometimes without reciprocity. Because you feel the way you feel, you continue to try, refusing to give up. Nothing wrong with trying, but you must know when to stop. Do not accept scraps!

Managing your Vomit

You must **manage** your interaction. You attempt to manage your interaction because you are so deeply intertwined with a person or situation. Regardless of the treatment you endured, you want the relationship to continue. So, you forget what has happened (to you) and you try to continue the relationship in some other form. *Let's just be friends.* Sometimes you will be successful and sometimes not.

If you must have certain people in your life, set boundaries. In some cases, first, you must forgive them. Then, set a boundary. In my second marriage, I forgave many times the way he treated me. Doing so enabled me to move forward with my objectives and ignore him when he attempted to distract me. Stay focused!

After I experienced my first heartbreak (Todd), it took me five years to forgive him. I only considered forgiving him because he wanted to be a part of my life. Then, he became my best friend. With my second heartbreak (George), things were a little more complicated. I forgave him several times too! I forgave him because I recognized that his own vomit invaded our relationship. But it was his inability, or lack of desire, to set boundaries that contributed to the demise of our relationship. I was alone in working to keep the relationship together. Establish limits!

Purging your Vomit

You must **purge** the *people or relationships* that have you bound. Loving someone allows them into your soul. Therefore, accepting that he or she is not healthy for you, and *releasing* them from your soul is even harder. But once your mind is made up, it becomes easier. Purging is similar to a colonic. Washing your colon cleanses the remnants of some healthy and unhealthy foods from your digestive system. Hypothetically, you will no longer crave those foods. Similarly, purging releases those memories of, and desires for, those unhealthy relationships and allows you to move on. Sometimes, God will purge those people or relationships for you!

I thought I was coping quite well when I decided to divorce my second husband. It was my idea to have that last dinner date. But when I departed from the restaurant and the uncontrollable tears began to flow, I was dumbfounded. Then years later, when I experienced that impactful pain in my stomach when confronted with the devastating truth about other people in my life, it was another form of purging for me. I understood that *my spirit* forced me to purge those people and relationships.

When you are in relationships, it is more than just your physical body that is involved or affected. *All of you* is involved and affected, including your inner spirit. Therefore, you must give yourself time to heal or purge when your relationships dissolve. Pray for release!

Surviving your Vomit

You can **survive** after purging. First, you must forgive yourself for allowing that person into your life in the first place. You can only heal after accepting responsibility for your role in the mess. Whether you let your guard down, were vulnerable, or you settled.

I was still angry about the times that I should have known better. I wished I could take back the part of myself that I had given in those relationships. I also wished I had been strong enough to fight the emotional attachments and physical desires that kept me bound like an idiot. How did I heal? I asked the Lord Jesus for help. Jesus will make you free!

Thriving After your Vomit

Know that you can **thrive** after surviving relationships. You are wiser and ready to start anew. Most importantly, you know to be specific in your prayers. But make sure you are prepared for a new relationship before you say your prayers. Sometimes God answers quickly. You need to be ready!

[12] Not that I have already obtained all this, or have already arrived at my goal, but I press on to take hold of that for which Christ Jesus took hold of me. [13] Brothers and sisters, I do not consider myself yet to have taken hold of it. But one thing I do: Forgetting what is behind and straining toward what is ahead, [14] I press on toward the goal to win the prize for which God has called me heavenward in Christ Jesus. (Philippians 3:12-14 NIV)

While you are experiencing the many challenges in life, you must pray without ceasing. Simply lay your cares and worries at the Lord's feet, and the answer will reveal itself. He is able!

Part VII – Monday Morning Quarterback

CHAPTER 33

Great Expectations

[7] "Ask and it will be given to you; seek and you will find; knock and the door will be opened to you. [8] For everyone who asks receives; the one who seeks finds; and to the one who knocks, the door will be opened. (Matthew 7:7-8 NIV)

I have poured my heart and soul into this book, hoping that you will learn something from my experiences. If I could do it all over again, I would pray first in all areas of my life! You see, my mother prayed for all her children. When you are spoiled, knowing you are covered by your mother's prayers, you do not think about praying for yourself. You accept what people give you, and then, "play the hand that is dealt to you."

I did not know God's plans for me. Therefore, whatever opportunities were presented to me, whether a job position or a relationship, I took advantage of them. I behaved as if it was another gift. Only after checking things out, did I decide whether it was for me or not. How else would I have known? I could have saved myself so much heartache and drama, and could have had so much more success, if I prayed to God first with some specific requests. He may have granted everything I asked for, or maybe not. I would rather have asked than not!

We are easily disappointed when things do not happen as expected. As a matter of fact, I am sure that is why we give up on our dreams so easily. We get tired of waiting for what we want, so we try to make the things in front of us work. When we give up and try to rush God when things do not happen quickly, we will never fully realize or receive what life's possibilities are for us.

I am a firm believer that God controls all things. When we tell Him exactly what we want, He will place the people we need on our paths to help us accomplish what we want, if it is His will. But if we do not know what we want, we will not recognize what we need to accomplish it, even when it is right in front of us. I am reminded of the story of Solomon.

> *[6] Solomon went up to the bronze altar before the Lord in the tent of meeting and offered a thousand burnt offerings on it. [7] That night God appeared to Solomon and said to him, "Ask for whatever you want me to give you." [8] Solomon answered God, "You have shown great kindness to David my father and have made me king in his place. [9] Now, Lord God, let your promise to my father David be confirmed, for you have made me king over a people who are as numerous as the dust of the earth. [10] Give me wisdom and knowledge, that I may lead this people, for who is able to govern this great people of yours?" [11] God said to Solomon, "Since this is your heart's desire and you have not asked for wealth, possessions or honor, nor for the death of your enemies, and since you have not asked for a long life but for wisdom and knowledge to govern my people over whom I have made you king, [12] therefore wisdom and knowledge will be given you. And I will also give you wealth, possessions and honor, such as no king who was before you ever had and none after you will have."*
> *(2 Chronicles 1:6-12 NIV)*

God gave Solomon an assignment – to "lead this people." Solomon asked God for wisdom and knowledge to complete the assignment that God gave him. God gave him that and way more than he asked for. Maybe Solomon did not ask for all that he needed, and God took care of that too!

God knows the desires of your heart. Maybe you are not asking God the right questions. What are your expectations? You need to give it some thought before you ask Him. Be specific because He may grant you that and way more than what you asked for too – if it is His will!

[26] In the same way, the Spirit helps us in our weakness. We do not know what we ought to pray for, but the Spirit himself intercedes for us through wordless groans. [27] And he who searches our hearts knows the mind of the Spirit, because the Spirit intercedes for God's people in accordance with the will of God.
(Romans 8:26-27 NIV)

I answered the call when I simply prayed with my friend on behalf of my mother. I accepted this mantle of prayer when led to pray for two more friends who called me while they were depressed and suicidal. After witnessing my mother pray for others, I knew that prayer could help my friends. As I told people that I had begun sharing prayers daily, they wanted to receive the prayers too. That was how my daily *Prayer Share* began.

When several recipients of the *Prayer Share* commented how much the prayers were helping them, I was encouraged to write my first book, *Prayers of My Mother*. As I began writing, I felt inspired as many of the short stories and anecdotes poured from within me and onto the pages. It was then that I knew it was my divine assignment. I learned from my readers the impact *Prayers of My Mother* had on their lives, and it was confirmation that writing the book was indeed my divine assignment. The Lord may have given you an assignment too, you just need to figure out what it is. Perhaps you are performing your divine assignment already and you just do not know it yet!

I knew that the Lord placed me on this path when three friends needed me, and I felt compelled to pray for them. You must be willing to receive prayer and believe in its power, for prayer to work in your life. I understood that if I helped at least one person believe in the power of prayer and they reaped the benefits of those prayers being answered, then I accomplished much.

Even when our prayers are not answered specifically, the relationship we build with God as a result of our prayers will help us understand that the result, His result, is way better! Therefore, I have even greater expectations for my life. I know the Lord is not finished with me – He is the potter; I am the clay.

[13] And I will do whatever you ask in my name, so that the Father may be glorified in the Son. [14] You may ask me for anything in my name, and I will do it.
(John 14:13-14 NIV)

Relationship Expectations

On my journey to this point in life, I reflect on some things that were said to me. My first husband said I was not going to find anyone else. That was not true. I have found quite a few somebodies. In the process, I have gained strength, wisdom, knowledge, clarity, self-awareness, and finally, discernment – to name a few. I now have specific criteria for my future mate.

My second husband told me that I needed to stop trying to be the man. I told him if he had been the man, I would not have had to be one. He also told me, "You think too much." How is it possible to think too much? I met another man who told me I was a diamond in the rough and had not met the right mate yet. The latter caused me to think, *who is the mate that can help make the diamond within me shine?*

[25] Husbands, love your wives, just as Christ loved the church and gave himself up for her [26] to make her holy, cleansing her by the washing with water through the word, [27] and to present her to himself as a radiant church, without stain or wrinkle or any other blemish, but holy and blameless. [28] In this same way, husbands ought to love their wives as their own bodies. He who loves his wife loves himself. (Ephesians 5:25-28 NIV)

I have had two husbands. I did not pray enough while with either of them. I knew our issues as husband and wife, and I communicated, verbally and non-verbally, hoping and believing that they would see the importance of changing our interactions. Many people in marriages wait until change happens. Sometimes change does happen, but at what cost? How long should we wait for change?

[18] The Lord God said, "It is not good for the man to be alone. I will make a helper suitable for him." (Genesis 2:18 NIV)

Where do we find the right mate? Is he in the church? Not all men who attend church and profess to be Christian are Christ-like. What are your criteria?

The most important criteria for me at this point in my life is that a mate support me on the path that God has placed me. I will recognize him because he will understand my purpose and not cause me conflict. Ultimately, I believe that God wants us with someone who is going to support and encourage the completion of the assignment that He has for us all.

So, when I am ready for a mate, I will lay my requests at the Lord's feet. My request will name specific qualities, characteristics, and values that I desire – with the understanding that the right mate will happen for me when *He* is ready.

CHAPTER 34

Faith and Hope

[20] We wait in hope for the Lord; he is our help and our shield. [21] In him our hearts rejoice, for we trust in his holy name. [22] May your unfailing love be with us, Lord, even as we put our hope in you. (Psalm 33:20-22 NIV)

This book is not the final chapter of my life. I hope for relationships that include trust, love, honesty, and respect – in all facets of my life. That is what having faith in God does. Faith gives us hope that things will get better, and we will live to see it. Never lose hope!

Be patient for whenever your time comes for whatever you are waiting on. Even when I did not pray for my situations and circumstances, I tried my best until my mind, body, and soul could do no more. Just imagine what could have happened if I had been praying the entire time, and not just when things were bad. I will never lose hope because I know that if God wants for me, whatever I am waiting for, it will happen. If God does not want for me, whatever I am waiting for, it is okay because I know He has something better planned for me.

[21] Many are the plans in a person's heart, but it is the Lord's purpose that prevails. (Proverbs 19:21 NIV)

My relationship with Ty was a personal experience that relates to the story of Job. Job was a very wealthy man. He and his family had everything they needed and could ever want. When the Lord allowed Satan to intervene into Job's life, even after Job lost everything – his possessions, sons, daughters, and his health, Job remained strong and faithful. He did not curse the Lord (*Job 1:11-12 NIV, Job 2:4-7 NIV*); and because of Job's faithfulness, the Lord blessed him twofold. He also gave him seven more sons and three more daughters. (*Job 42:10 NIV, Job 42:13-15 NIV*)

Like Job, the Lord had blessed me tremendously, even though I had not achieved the level of faith that Job had. Initially, Ty's fake persona was my fantasy. I thought he was just another one of God's many blessings in my life. But God allowed Ty to enter my life at the most inopportune time, when I was most vulnerable – heartbroken and disappointed, to bring me to my knees. Nevertheless, the Lord continuously provided discernment that Ty was not for me, and I ignored it.

The devil intervened and took over my common sense. Ty's deceit and insensitivity towards women proved that sexual intimacy for some men was just a necessary biological function, void of love or any special intimacy that women can relate to. Relationships were such a game to Ty that it forced me to see that I had lost touch with reality. There were games being played and I was too trusting. It was the biggest mistake of my life. I wanted to be angry with God, but I could not because He protected me when I let this stranger into my life.

When the Lord finally spoke to Job, He reminded him of who He is. *(Job 38-41)* Then Job said what we all have learned at some point in our lives.

[2] "I know that you can do all things; no purpose of yours can be thwarted. (Job 42:2 NIV)

The story of Job, although a poignant and devastating one, is also one of faith and hope. By no means was my Ty story of the same magnitude in comparison to Job's, yet it involved the intrusion into my life of the devil's spawn that Ty was. Even when my common sense was gone, the Lord remained with me, nagging me until I finally listened and saw Ty for who and what he was.

I was so angry with myself after the relationship with Ty, that I asked God why He allowed that relationship to happen. He answered, "It was for this." "This" being the most important chapter of my life, what I am doing now for the Kingdom of Heaven. It was that message that helped me to forgive myself and heal; and accept my calling to fulfill the assignment God has for me. I know that He will continue to give me the tools I need to fulfill my destiny.

[11] In him we were also chosen, having been predestined according to the plan of him who works out everything in conformity with the purpose of his will, [12] in order that we, who were the first to put our hope in Christ, might be for the praise of his glory. (Ephesians 1:11-12 NIV)

What exactly am I doing for the Kingdom of Heaven, you ask? I am sharing the Word, the love of God, my stories of vulnerability, and prayers. Finally, I share the faith that was instilled in me by my praying mother, so that you will have hope and believe in God and the power of prayer, too!

In my first book, *Prayers of My Mother*, I gave you practical application of the scriptures, enabling you to apply them in present-day life. The Bible transcends time and I encouraged you to take a thought-provoking look at the Word, leaving you with clarity and a deeper understanding of the Bible. As I studied the Bible, I recognized how the same flaws, mistakes, and regrets that we experience today were also experienced by people during Biblical times; and that the same parallel choices, rewards, and consequences still apply.

My mother introduced me to the Spirit of the Lord as a teenager and taught me the power of prayer. When my mother explained her ability to hear Him, I was astonished. How can that be? But when I began to hear the quiet but very audible Voice, during pivotal moments of my life, I understood.

In this book, I give you specific and relatable life experiences, admitting to things that most people are afraid to admit, just so you know that you are not alone in life's struggles, including heartbreak. I also introduced the Spirit of the Lord through my stories to help you recognize Him in your own life. I offered realistic guidance and inspiration to help you purge, heal, and focus on what is important in your life. In essence, I suggested unique ways to reconnect with God and celebrate faith in the modern day. He is always available for spiritual reinforcement – by any means necessary.

I want you to have faith and hope. I was transparent about my trials and tribulations, challenges, failures, and triumphs; and demonstrated my faith in God through the ability to hope and pray throughout my circumstances. It only takes a little bit of faith to believe that prayer changes things. Remember, nothing is too hard for the Lord!

[6] Humble yourselves, therefore, under God's mighty hand, that he may lift you up in due time. [7] Cast all your anxiety on him because he cares for you. (1 Peter 5:6-7 NIV)

I have hope for my future. God continued to bless me, even when I did not listen; and I have no complaints. Now that I have learned how to listen, I will let the Spirit of the Lord continue to lead me on the path He has laid before me. My life is not over, and I hope I assisted you with yours. Am I winning? Absolutely!

[1] Now faith is confidence in what we hope for and assurance about what we do not see. (Hebrews 11:1 NIV)

EPILOGUE

[11] As a dog returns to its vomit, so fools repeat their folly. (Proverbs 26:11 NIV)

Admittedly, I have eaten my vomit, and it was not a pleasant experience. Consequently, I know the importance of having to purge some things and people from my life. Purging is not something I want to do repeatedly. I am reminded of one definition for insanity: extreme folly or unreasonableness. After reading this book, you will recognize if you have eaten, are eating, or were thinking about eating your vomit!

You will interact with people during your life. *Don't Eat Your Vomit!* is a playbook reviewing the different phases of my life, along with the fumbles, interceptions, touchdowns, and instant replays. At some point, you will experience career or relationship vomit, or both.

You tolerate so much from people hoping they will change. Eventually you realize that you accomplished nothing because you cannot change them. Don't eat the vomit you can't change! So, what will you do? Will you manage or purge it?

From the Author

Don't Eat Your Vomit! was extremely difficult to write because I wrestled with sharing my challenges, especially the personal relationships. Frankly, I decided to omit writing about my marriage woes, which was ludicrous because they are the crux of this book. The day after I made that decision, I heard the Spirit of the Lord say, "Yes, you will write about them!"

I have a big heart. I want to believe in and trust people, but it has been to my own detriment. Too many people are selfish and have ulterior motives in all that they do. Those same people are often very close to you or want to be.

As with my first book, *Prayers of My Mother*, I am again transparent regarding my experiences; not only to encourage, console and heal, but to also help people release the things that have them bound. I hope that *Don't Eat Your Vomit!* inspires many to recognize the behaviors we consistently repeat with others and those that are consistently repeated with us. Most important is understanding that if some of those behaviors are unhealthy, they will negatively interfere with our healthy relationships and even other areas of our lives – the relationships with our children or extended family members, even our careers.

Specifically, I have also heard the Spirit of the Lord speak to me, always softly but firm, when at a crossroad with certain people or situations in my life. Once, I began rethinking divorce, believing that I had another bright idea to help the state of my marriage. As I thought of an alternative, not realizing I had tried it before, the Spirit reminded me, "Didn't you do that already?" He will only let you wallow in your mess for so long before He pulls you up! You can hear Him too, but you must learn *Listening with a Different Ear*.

About My Mother

As Christians, it is our duty to fulfill the mission of the church. Currently, I carry out this mission by spreading the Word of God through Scripture and prayer. In addition to the Holy Spirit, prayer is also one of the most powerful access tools and gifts the Lord has given us. It is our direct means of communication and continues to give to ourselves and others; it glorifies God.

Although I am aware that many have access to these gifts, reflection has made me keenly aware that ministry runs in my blood. My grandmother, Margaret Rabb Riggs, was born in March 1890. Her father was a German Jew, who forced himself on her African American mother, a South Carolina native. Grandma Riggs was ostracized by her mother's side of the family due to her unique physical features.

Grandma Riggs eventually relocated to Knoxville, Tennessee, my mother's birthplace. Grandma Riggs had six girls - Willie, Doretha, Agnes, Glodene, Margaret, and Flora. Somehow, they eventually migrated to Miami, FL. To the best of my knowledge, this is where my grandmother began utilizing her spiritual gift – prophecy. The gift of prophecy is an extraordinary gift because it enables those who have it to speak God's Word with authority. This is a powerful tool amongst believers and non-believers as it confirms God's omnipresence.

In the 50's and 60's, Grandma Riggs was known in Liberty City, FL as the Barefoot Prophet. My older brothers, Charles and Winston, would tell stories from their youth of picking glass from my grandmother's feet because she insisted on walking barefooted.

Winston told me that he did not recall her being a member of any specific church, yet she held weekly Bible studies on Wednesday evenings and Saturday mornings when she could. Those familiar with her would remember her as being plainly dressed in a white calf length dress that buttoned down the front. Winston also recalls that she sometimes wore white hats with a long veil in the back. Grandma Riggs' preference for white garments was influenced by her religion and she would only be seen wearing white as she fulfilled her mission by praying for the sick and shut in (***Revelations 3:4-5***). Although Grandma Riggs died in 1971 when I was only nine years old, I know that my ministry began with her, or perhaps even with someone who came before her.

My mother, Margaret Frances Riggs, was born in January 1927. She had six children, three girls and three boys – Charles, Winston, Agnes, Frederick, Carolyn, and Anthenisia. She was a devout Christian and minister of prayer, who followed in her mother's footsteps. Not only did my mother pray for the sick and shut in as did her mother, she was also a Healer. This is a beautiful gift as it relies heavily on one's faith and trust in God. Healings are important to ministry as they draw people closer to God. My mother once told my younger sister that the Spirit told her there would be none like her. Although I am not sure if the gift of healing alone triggered my mother to begin praying for others, I know that my decision to step in to pray for one when my mother could not has forever changed my life.

TESTIMONIALS

...Reflective and thought provoking. Forced me to reflect on my life, relationships, jobs, friendships, and family; and examine how I repeated and resolved certain scenarios. Most importantly, if I am continuing the same patterns in my life today, the book showed me how to release them – especially if harmful.
Rhonda D., Greensboro, NC

The story drew me in from the beginning, and I did not put it down until I finished! I dated someone while in my 20s who never committed. Those were my best years, and I didn't have time to waste. He said something I will never forget, "No time is ever wasted if you get something out of it." So, even though we've all eaten our own vomit...as my grandmother used to say, "Bought sense is better than told!" *N. Holmes, Lithonia, GA*

Triggered self-reflection of relationship experiences long buried. If we don't deal head on with our poor choices, our daughters will have unnecessary struggles and pain. There are serious things we must tell our daughters... *Paulette J., Plymouth Meeting, PA*

Definitely recognized my own vomit! The men were dishonest because they were intimidated by the author. Women believe that men want to be in a relationship – some are content in non-exclusive relationships. The author tried too hard to see the good in everyone. We cannot help or change someone who is unwilling to do so. *A. Johnson, Jonesboro, GA*

Vomit flowing like a river! I applaud the author for her transparency in sharing the raw, bad, and ugly vomit experiences of her career and personal relationships. Certainly, an epiphany that caused me to do much soul-searching. *A. Jones, Chicago, IL*

Very inspiring! Helped me identify games men play. I also learned how to pray for strength when going through tough times on the job, in relationships, or just in general. This book will help you identify patterns in people, so you don't make the same mistakes repeatedly. Hard to put down and full of life lessons! *M. Lowe, Ruskin, FL*

TESTIMONIALS Cont'd

I didn't want to put the book down! We are not alone in making the same mistakes multiple times. This book includes Bible verse references to assist us in our mistake-filled journey through life. I reflected on my relationship vomit especially when I was trying to find my husband. I can now see the vomit in one of my daughters' lives, but she refuses to rely on God to assist her in making the right decisions. *Deborah M., Columbia, SC*

It's a page-turner! A jewelry box filled with gems – life lessons! Words to live by...a handbook to avoid unnecessary consumption of one's own vomit. Inspirational to say the least! *F. Peck, Tampa, FL*

About My Team

Yeudele Allen is an author and serves as executive director, New Vision Christian Church, Morrow, GA. Yeudele's philosophy is know truth, know peace; sow truth, grow peace; no truth, no peace. Truth settles the whole matter. Her favorite scripture is Philippians 4:8.

Marlené Carter is an author and veteran who served 21 years in the Army to include a tour in Iraq. Her favorite scripture is Proverbs 3:3.

Deborah McCutchan has been married for more than 31 years and is the mother of 2 grown daughters. She is an animal lover and has many cats and 2 horses. Deborah is a financial advisor and has a passion for helping people realize their dreams. Her favorite scripture is 1 Corinthians 16:13.

Caroiya A. Williams is an author, educator, and entrepreneur with a zest for the lighter side of life. Writing is her greatest passion and her quest for knowledge and achievement is unparalleled. Her favorite Scripture is Psalm 23:4.

INDEX